Routledge Revivals

Ceylon

I0121708

First published in 1952, *Ceylon* is a one-volume history of Ceylon, primarily intended for the non-Ceylonese reader who has no special knowledge of Asia. People, places, and dates have been kept to a minimum in the book. The focus has been on the evolution of a nation and the ideas which have influenced its growth.

The volume outlines the history ranging from pre-historic period through independence in 1948. Beginning with a brief introduction of Ceylon and its people, the author discusses the arrival of the Sinhalese; Tamil invasions; Portuguese and Dutch period; the British conquest from 1795–1815; Kandyan War, Colebrooke Commission and Lord Torrington's Administration; and the development, consolidation, and the struggle for independence. He concludes with a short essay on Ceylon and the future. This book will appeal to anyone with an interest in the history of Asia and to students and researchers of Asian studies and history.

Ceylon

Sydney D. Bailey

Routledge
Taylor & Francis Group

First published in 1952
by Hutchinson & Co. (Publishers) Ltd

This edition first published in 2024 by Routledge
4 Park Square, Milton Park, Abingdon, Oxon, OX14 4RN

and by Routledge
605 Third Avenue, New York, NY 10017

Routledge is an imprint of the Taylor & Francis Group, an informa business

Publisher's Note
The publisher has gone to great lengths to ensure the quality of this reprint but points
out that some imperfections in the original copies may be apparent.

Disclaimer
The publisher has made every effort to trace copyright holders and welcomes
correspondence from those they have been unable to contact.

A Library of Congress record exists under LCCN: 52010348

ISBN: 978-1-032-87496-8 (hbk)
ISBN: 978-1-003-53291-0 (ebk)
ISBN: 978-1-032-87497-5 (pbk)

Book DOI 10.4324/9781003532910

CEYLON

by

SYDNEY D. BAILEY

ASSISTANT DIRECTOR OF
THE HANSARD SOCIETY

HUTCHINSON'S UNIVERSITY LIBRARY

Hutchinson House, Stratford Place, W.1.

New York   Melbourne   Sydney   Cape Town

First published · 1952

Printed in Great Britain by
William Brendon and Son, Ltd.
The Mayflower Press (late of Plymouth)
at Bushey Mill Lane
Watford, Herts.

CONTENTS

PREFACE

I DO not know of any book which attempts to provide the non-Ceylonese reader with a one-volume history of Ceylon. There are a number of excellent text-books written primarily for the Ceylonese student, but these all assume that the reader has some knowledge of Ceylon, its peoples and its languages. This book has been written for the intelligent citizen who has no special knowledge of Asia. Persons, places, and dates have been kept to a minimum. The emphasis, rather, has been on the evolution of a nation and the ideas which have influenced its growth.

I have taken the liberty of modernizing the punctuation, spelling, and capitalization in a number of quotations from Robert Knox and other early writers.

I would like to express my gratitude to the following, who read all or part of the first draft of the book and suggested improvements: Senator Sir Ukwatte Jayasundera, Sir Ivor Jennings, Sir Drummond Shiels, and Mr. S. A. Pakeman. I alone, of course, am responsible for the contents of the book. May I also thank the staff of the British Museum Reading Room, the Colonial Office Library, and the Public Record Office who were unfailingly helpful.

November 1951.   S. D. B.

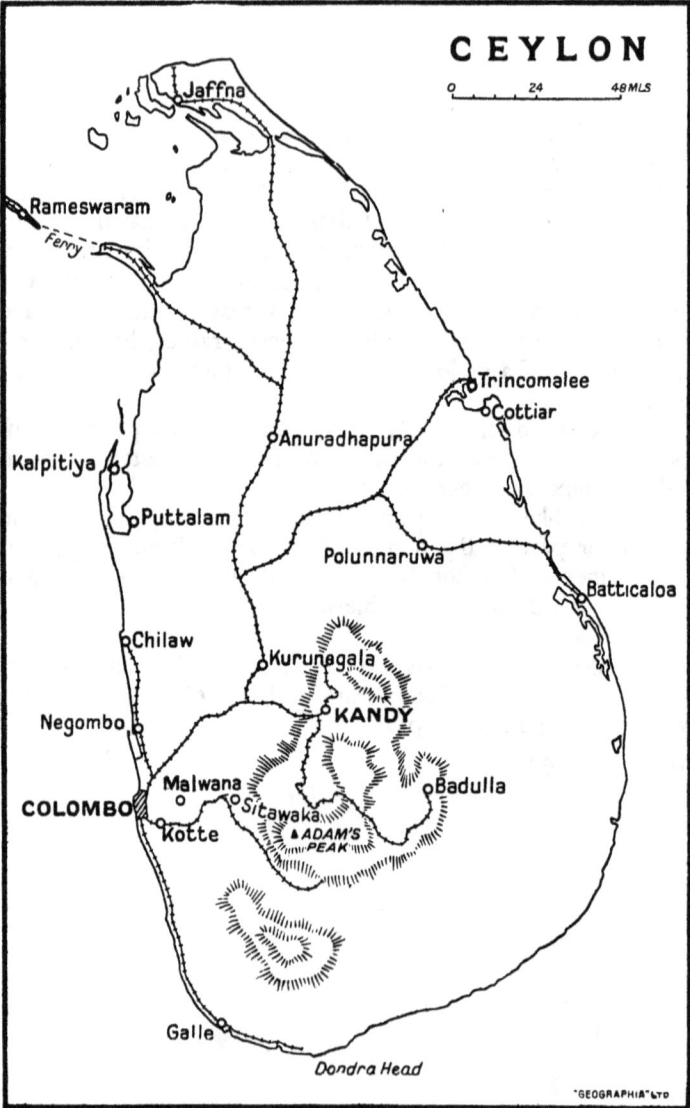

CEYLON

0   24   48 MLS

Jaffna

Rameswaram

Ferry

Trincomalee

Cottiar

Anuradhapura

Kalpitiya

Puttalam

Polunnaruwa

Batticaloa

Chilaw

Kurunagala

KANDY

Negombo

Malwana

Badulla

COLOMBO

Sitawaka

Kotte

▲ ADAM'S PEAK

Galle

Dondra Head

"GEOGRAPHIA" LTD

CHAPTER I

CEYLON AND ITS PEOPLE

What though the spicy breezes
Blow soft o'er Ceylon's isle;
Though every prospect pleases,
And only man is vile:
In vain with lavish kindness
The gifts of God are sown;
The heathen, in his blindness,
Bows down to wood and stone.

So wrote Reginald Heber, in 1819, though he had never in fact been to Ceylon. He visited the island six years later when he was Bishop of Calcutta and changed "Ceylon's isle" to "Java's isle".

But many people must have been first introduced to Ceylon through these lines, and it is pertinent to ask whether they give a fair picture of Ceylon and its people. Bishop Heber, when he wrote this missionary hymn, had a frankly didactic purpose. He wanted to persuade his hearers that God's beautiful handiwork was being marred by ignorant heathens and that the position could only be remedied by supporting Christian missions. It was, indeed, a noble purpose, and Bishop Heber was no more guilty of dishonesty than was Shakespeare when he put into the mouth of John of Gaunt, Duke of Lancaster, the inspiring words about England: "This other Eden, demi-paradise. . . . This precious stone set in a silver sea. . . . This blessed plot, this earth, this realm, this England."

Most travellers who have visited Ceylon have been at once impressed with the beauty and colour of the country. Sir Emerson Tennent begins his classic book on Ceylon, published a century ago, with these words: "Ceylon, from whatever direction it may be approached, unfolds a scene of loveliness and grandeur unsurpassed, if it be rivalled, by any land in the universe." Such unrestrained admiration is typical. The modern traveller, no less than his predecessors down the centuries, echoes Reginald Heber's sentiment that "every prospect pleases".

Ceylon is a pearl-shaped island, lying in the tropics off the southern tip of India. Its area is approximately 25,000 square miles, that is, about the same as Tasmania, the American State of West Virginia, or the Republic of Ireland. Early writers greatly exaggerated its size. Marco Polo thought it had a circumference of 2,400 miles, about four times as great as the actual circumference.

Ceylon's strategic position in the Indian Ocean has been of great importance in influencing the island's history. It has always been very much of a cosmopolitan country, and Chinese, Indian, Malay, Arab, African and European immigrants have lived and worked side by side with the native inhabitants. Four of the great religions of the world have substantial numbers of adherents in Ceylon. The variety and richness of Ceylon's cultural heritage is due in large measure to the clash of ideas from three continents.

Yet the very fact of Ceylon's strategic importance has made it a tempting prey for foreign invaders. "The importance of Ceylon is such that, if English troops captured that island, its recapture would be more important than all other conquests wherewith one could begin a war in India." So wrote the French Admiral Suffren in 1782.

Ceylon's history is, indeed, a long record of foreign invasion. Up till the end of the first millennium of the Christian era the invaders were mainly Aryans from the Hindu civilization of North India. Then for five centuries the attacks came from the Tamil-speaking peoples of South India. From the beginning of the sixteenth century to the middle of the twentieth, Ceylon —or the major part of it—was a colony of a European power, first of Portugal, then of Holland, finally of Britain. Today the country is independent, freely associated with the other nations of the British Commonwealth.

The population numbers just over seven million (1950). The people can be classified in various ways. For instance, one can say that 50 per cent are engaged in agriculture, 10 per cent are engaged in industry, 7 per cent are traders, and so on. Or the people can be classified by religion and one can say that

64 per cent are Buddhists, 19 per cent are Hindus, 9 per cent are Christians, and 6 per cent are Moslems. Or they can be classified by communities and one can say that 69 per cent are Sinhalese, 11 per cent are Ceylon Tamils, 12 per cent are Indian Tamils, and 6 per cent are Moors. Or one can get down to more human characteristics and say that some of the people are cheerful and some are unhappy, some are rich and some are poor, some are energetic and some are lazy, some are intelligent and some are stupid. The important thing about a person is not the category in which he appears in a census table but his personality, the environment into which he is born, the way he lives. In all really important respects, indeed, the peoples of the world share similar experiences.

Thus in recounting the history of Ceylon we shall not be concerned solely with dynasties and kings, with invasions and conquests, but with the movement of ideas and with the effect of historic events on the lives of ordinary people.

*　　*　　*　　*　　*

Ceylon is mainly an agricultural country. The most important home-produced exports are tea (forming 65 per cent of the value of the total in 1949), rubber (13 per cent in 1949), and coco-nut products (19 per cent in 1949). These three commodities, it will be seen, provide almost the entire total of the island's exports. The balance is made up in the main of other agricultural products such as areca nuts and cinnamon. Although only a small country, Ceylon produces about one-fifth of the world's tea, one-tenth of the world's coco-nut products, 14 per cent of the world's plumbago (graphite), and 7 per cent of the world's rubber.

Only one person in ten is employed in manufacturing industries, transport and mining, whereas in a highly industrialized country like Britain about half the working population is so employed. This fact has influenced the character of the people. Life, for the majority, is simple and unhurried. The peasant cultivates what he needs for himself and his family, and sells any surplus in order to supply his modest needs.

There are few large towns. Colombo, the capital, had a

population of a little over 350,000 in 1946. The other well-known places have few inhabitants. Jaffna with just over 60,000 people, and Galle and Kandy with about 50,000 people each, are the only other towns of any size. Nine people out of ten live in the countryside.

The culture of Ceylon has been greatly influenced by its proximity to India and by the fact that many of the inhabitants have racial, religious or linguistic affinities with the Indian peoples. As in other parts of the world, the development of a national culture has been closely associated with religion. The great historical chronicles such as the *Mahavamsa*, the frescoes at Sigiriya, the recently restored Circular Shrine at Medirigiriya, the temples and sculptures in the ancient cities which for centuries lay buried beneath a tangled mass of earth and vegetation, these were all works of art created by pious men who wanted to give expression to their inner faith.

The first art was essentially Buddhist in character. Then during the period of the Tamil invasions, from the eleventh to the fifteenth centuries, Hindu influences were introduced and mingled with the earlier tradition. European art has been a factor during the past four and a half centuries, but its influence has not been entirely happy. Only during the twentieth century has there been a renaissance of genuinely indigenous art.

The literature of the West—and especially English literature—has had a profound influence. English is the language of officialdom and the business community: it is the medium of instruction for the privileged classes, and most of the best-known Ceylonese writers have written in English.

The national unity in which the people of Ceylon take a just pride has been created from many diverse elements. This book recounts some of the events in Ceylon's history which have contributed to the diversity.

CHAPTER II

THE ARRIVAL OF THE SINHALESE

All historical books which contain no lies are extremely tedious.—Anatole France.

THE main difficulty which confronts the person who wants to learn about the early history of Ceylon is to separate fact from fable, truth from tradition. This is partly because there is so much more of fable than of fact, partly because fable—thinly disguised as fact—is so entertaining. What, for instance, could be more delightful than this story of the island's origin which comes to us from Fa Hsien, a Chinese Buddhist priest who visited Ceylon in the fifth century of the Christian era?

"This country was not originally inhabited by human beings, but only by devils and dragons, with whom the merchants of the neighbouring countries traded by barter. At the time of the barter the devils did not appear, but set out their valuables with the prices attached. The merchants then gave goods according to the prices marked and took away the goods they wanted. And from the merchants going backwards and forwards and some stopping there, the attractions of the place became widely known, and people went thither in great numbers, so that it became a great nation."

Or what could be more plausible than the Portuguese tradition of the origin of Ceylon which is recorded by Robert Knox, an Englishman who was a prisoner on the island during the seventeenth century?

"An ancient King of China had a son who, during his father's reign, proved so very harsh and cruel unto the people that they, being afraid he might prove a tyrant if he came to the crown, desired the King to banish him, and that

13

he might never succeed. This that King, to please the people,
granted. And so put him with certain attendants into a ship
and turned them forth upon the winds to seek their fortune.
The first shore they were cast upon was this island: which
they seated themselves on and peopled it. But to me nothing
is more improbable than this story."

The early history of Ceylon is redolent with such unlikely
tales. Fa Hsien's story of dragons and devils is so manifestly
mythical that we enjoy it for what it is. But as fiction and fact
merge, our task becomes more difficult. Epic poems and chronicles, designed as much to inspire as to inform, purport to tell
the early history of Ceylon. The task of distinguishing what
was intended to inspire from what was intended to inform is
well nigh impossible for the modern student.

The early history of the island comes to us from a variety
of sources. The most important Ceylonese source is the
Mahavamsa. This is a chronicle, compiled by Buddhist priests,
describing the events in the life of the island which seemed
important to the authors. Supplementing the *Mahavamsa* are
other more fragmentary chronicles and allegedly historical books.

Indian legends about Ceylon, in which fact and fiction
merge, should also be noticed. There is, for example, the
great Hindu epic poem, the *Ramayana*. This tells of Rama, an
Indian prince, whose wife Sita is abducted by the demon-king
of Ceylon. Rama sets out to rescue her and with the help of
the monkey-god builds a causeway from the Indian mainland
to Ceylon. He then crosses with an army and frees Sita. Some
identify Rama as an incarnation of Vishnu, the god of protection, and Sita as an incarnation of Lakshmi, the goddess of
beauty and fortune. Rama and Sita are to this day worshipped
by the Ramats, a North Indian Hindu sect.

In addition to these chronicles and epic poems, we have a
few accounts left by foreign visitors to Ceylon. The existence
of Ceylon was known to early Roman and Greek writers, though
its exact position was uncertain and its size much exaggerated.
The first European to visit Ceylon, so far as is known, was a
pilot of the fleet of Alexander the Great. He visited the island
during the fourth century B.C.

About the year 300 B.C. the king of Macedonia sent as ambassador to the court of the Indian emperor a man named Megasthenes. This man lived at Patna and apparently wrote a full description of India and the neighbouring countries. The original work has not survived, but it is quoted frequently by later Greek writers. Megasthenes mentioned Ceylon, described the inhabitants, referred to some of the animals found on the island, and wrote of the gems and gold which, even at that early date, were exported.

Other Greek astronomers, geographers and scientists of the third and second centuries B.C.—including Eratosthenes, Hipparchus, and Artemidorus—mention Ceylon. Their works have been lost, but they are quoted by later writers. Strabo, the Greek geographer who wrote at the beginning of the first century of the Christian era, mentions Ceylon. Pliny the Elder, writing a few years later, collected a good deal of information from a Roman customs official who was shipwrecked off Ceylon and stayed there several months. The information no doubt seemed remarkable at the time but strikes the modern reader as prosaic. The island was apparently prosperous, the soil fertile, the people contented, and the form of government reported to be mild. The fullest early European account of Ceylon comes from Ptolemy, the Greek geographer, who wrote his *System of Geography* in the second century A.D. His map of Ceylon was remarkably accurate and was used extensively by later writers, as well as by mariners.

*   *   *   *   *

The first King of Ceylon, according to the account in the *Mahavamsa*, was named Vijaya. His grandmother is said to have been an Indian princess who, "desiring the joy of independent life", left home and joined a travelling caravan. The caravan was attacked by a lion, but the princess had no fear and caressed the animal. "The lion, roused to fiercest passion by her touch, took her upon his back and bore her with all speed to his cave, and there he was united with her, and from this union with him the princess in time bore twin children, a son and a daughter." When he was sixteen years old the son carried off his mother and sister. The lion went in pursuit of his family, ravaging the countryside, until the local king offered a reward to anyone who would destroy the animal. The son slew the lion with an arrow and claimed the reward. At this time the king was dying and the son was acclaimed king in his stead. He married his sister who "bore twin sons sixteen times". The eldest son, Vijaya, "was of evil conduct" and the people demanded his death. The king decided to get rid of Vijaya and sent him away. He departed with 700 companions, together with their wives and children, and eventually landed in Ceylon which was then inhabited by demons. He took a demon woman for his wife, and with her supernatural skill destroyed the other demons. His followers asked him to become their king, but Vijaya refused "unless a maiden of noble house were consecrated as queen". Anxious to have Vijaya as king, his companions sent to India and secured a princess who became his queen. After his marriage he forsook his evil ways and ruled in peace and righteousness for thirty-eight years. His demon wife fled with her children to the mountains, and their descendants became known as Veddas.

There are several variants of this story, which has many parallels in western mythology. Its main interest arises from the fact that the Sanskrit word for lion is *Sinha*, and the Aryan inhabitants of Ceylon are known as Sinhalese. The word Ceylon itself is derived from *Sinha*.

The Veddas, who are described in the story of Vijaya as descendants of the demon inhabitants, were almost certainly the first inhabitants of Ceylon. They were a primitive nomadic people, racially akin to some of the jungle tribes of South India and the aborigines of Australia. There are today only a few hundred pure Veddas living in Ceylon.

It seems certain that during the sixth or fifth century B.C. Aryan invaders landed in Ceylon and subjugated the primitive Veddas. The story of Vijaya in its various forms is no doubt a legend based on this historical event. These Aryans, from whom the modern Sinhalese are descended, were a more civilized people than the Veddas. They led a settled life and were familiar with simple agricultural methods. There were in Ceylon, in 1949, more than five million Sinhalese, mainly descendants of these early Aryan invaders: they form about 70 per cent of the total population of the island.

There are traditions, recorded in the *Mahavamsa*, that the Buddha, who lived in the sixth century B.C., visited Ceylon several times. On the third occasion he is said to have left the imprint of his foot on the mountain known as Adam's Peak. "When the Teacher, compassionate to the whole world, had preached the doctrine there," record the chroniclers, "he rose, the Master, and left the traces of his footsteps plain to sight." But Adam's Peak, as its name implies, has other religious associations besides Buddhist and is regarded as holy by Moslems, Hindus, and Christians. It has always fascinated foreign visitors to Ceylon. Fa Hsien, the Chinese Buddhist priest, recounts how the Buddha, wishing "to convert the wicked dragons", placed one foot on the royal city and the other on Adam's Peak, thus demonstrating his divine power. Marco Polo, who visited Ceylon towards the end of the thirteenth century, tells us that at the top of the mountain was a tomb which, "the idolators" asserted, contained the remains of the Buddha but which in reality contained the remains of Adam who had landed on Ceylon when he was cast out of paradise. Friar Odoric, who passed through Ceylon about the year 1321, also visited Adam's Peak "where, the inhabitants of that region report, Adam mourned for his son Abel the space of 500 years. In the midst of this mountain," he continues, "there is a most beautiful plain wherein is a little lake containing a great amount of water which the inhabitants report to have come from the tears of Adam and Eve. However, I proved that to be false because I saw the water flow into the lake." John of Marignolli, the papal legate to the court of the Great Khan, visited Ceylon about the year 1350 and describes Adam's Peak as "the highest mountain on the face of the earth". He mentions the place where the footprint can be seen and describes the marble house which Adam "made with his own hands". The inhabitants told him that the great flood had not covered the peak, so Adam's house had survived. Marignolli also refers to Adam's tears, but in his version these had miraculously become precious stones.

*   *   *   *   *

In the third century B.C. Asoka became Emperor of India. He spent the early years of his reign in subduing the part of India now known as Orissa, but he later became filled with remorse for the suffering he had caused and became a devout Buddhist. He sent emissaries including his son Mahinda, to Ceylon, and the Sinhalese king and many of his subjects embraced the new religion. More than 90 per cent of the Sinhalese community are today Buddhists.

Not many years after the introduction of Buddhism to Ceylon, the island was again invaded from India. The invaders were Tamil-speaking Hindus from the Chola country (what is now the Madras province of India) and they were led by a nobleman called Elara. There had probably been other Tamil-speaking immigrants before this. There was no doubt considerable intermarriage between these Tamil people and the Sinhalese, but the fact that the Tamils were Hindus and the Sinhalese were Buddhists tended to keep the two communities apart. The descendants of these and later Tamil-speaking Hindu immigrants and invaders are known today as Ceylon Tamils, and number about 800,000: they are still predominantly Hindu by religion.

According to the *Mahavamsa*, Elara ruled as king for forty-four years "with even justice towards friend and foe". "At the head of his bed he had a bell hung up with a long rope so that those who desired a judgment at law might ring it." The *Dipavamsa*, another Buddhist chronicle, records that "this incomparable monarch reigned righteously, avoiding the four evil paths of lust, hatred, fear, and ignorance". In the end he was slain by a certain Dutthagamani, the 'Bad Prince'. This prince had an unruly disposition and left his home as a youth. He collected his own army and defeated the Tamil invaders, slaying the King Elara with a dart. He then united the whole of Ceylon under one rule. After his victory was complete he returned to his palace where, sitting on the terrace, "adorned, lighted with fragrant lamps and filled with many a perfume, magnificent with nymphs in the guise of dancing girls, while he rested on his soft and fair couch, covered with costly draperies, he looked back upon his glorious victory and, great though it was, knew no joy remembering that thereby was wrought the destruction of millions". And the pious Buddhist chronicler adds this comment: "Should a man think on the hosts of human beings murdered for greed in countless myriads, and should he carefully keep in mind the evil that arises from this, and should he also very carefully keep in mind that mortality is the killer of all, then he will shortly win peace of mind and freedom from suffering."

*   *   *   *   *

The history of Ceylon until the end of the first millenium of the Christian era is known only in fragmentary form. The story is one of successive invasions from India, interspersed with internal struggles between the Sinhalese kings who controlled the northern part of the island and rival chieftains who established themselves in the south. Originally the Sinhalese capital was at Anuradhapura, but it was moved to Polonnaruva in A.D. 760. It is not possible in this book to describe in detail the invasions and battles, the dynastic rivalries and royal quarrels of these centuries. Indeed, the catalogue of dates and names and places has no special significance. All that we can do is to refer briefly to a few of the more notable figures and events in the turbulent history of those times, and then describe the kind of society which existed in Ceylon during this period.

At the beginning of the third century A.D. a king called Vera Tissa came to the throne. He is said to have abolished torture and maiming: he was a pious man, according to the *Mahavamsa*, "keeping the heretics in check". During the reign of his grandson there was some sort of dynastic quarrel, the king was slain, and another branch of the royal family seized the throne. The usurping king's son, Siri Sangabo, came to the throne about the year A.D. 250. He was a saintly man and, according to the *Rajavaliya*, ended a serious drought "by the influence of his observance of moral precepts". During his reign a certain Golu Aba, brother of the king who had been murdered during the dynastic dispute a few years earlier, attempted to regain the throne for his own branch of the family. Siri Sangabo seems to have been a pacifist, for it is recorded that he offered no resistance and became a monk. Golu Aba,

having ascended the throne, offered a reward for the head of
Siri Sangabo. Many heads were taken to the king by persons
who claimed the reward, but none of these was that of the
ex-king. Hearing how many murders were being committed
for the sake of wealth, the pious Siri Sangabo is said to have
severed his own head, which was taken to the new king, Golu
Aba.

Golu Aba was himself a righteous man, according to the
chronicles, though he had trouble with priests who held heretical doctrines. It is recorded in the *Dipavamsa* that he erected
many religious buildings and "having constructed a royal
palace, a great, delightful building, gave it to the Buddhist
priests". He built "a cloister for monks given to meditation",
"an incomparable stone altar round the Bo tree," and "a very
costly triumphal arch". His brother Mahasena, who became
king in 274, is remembered for his irrigation works. His reign
was disturbed by religious controversies, and the *Mahavamsa*
chroniclers are highly critical of him: they describe him as
"unwise" and say that he "wrought many a deed of wrong".
The *Rajavaliya* records that he "employed demons in his
service". The writers of the *Dipavamsa* ascribe his sinful life
to evil companions: "therefore one should fly far from intercourse with wicked men".

It was during the reign of Mahasena's son that the sacred
Tooth Relic of the Buddha was taken to Ceylon from India.
"A Brahmin woman," records the *Culavamsa*, "brought to
Anuradhapura from the Kalinga country [the modern Orissa]
the Tooth Relic of the Great Sage. . . . The ruler received it
with reverence, paid it the highest honours, and laid it in an
urn of pure crystal." The story is different in the *Rajavaliya*:
according to this account, the King of Kalinga had given instructions that, in the event of his death in battle, the Tooth
Relic was to be taken to Ceylon by his daughter and her
husband.

The Tooth Relic was supposed to be one of the actual
teeth of the Buddha and was the object of great veneration
and worship. It was believed to have miraculous powers, and
in the course of time the tradition grew up that whoever
possessed it was the lawful king of the island. Fa Hsien tells

us that it was kept in a special shrine at the capital. Ten days before the middle of the third moon the king caused an orator dressed in royal apparel to mount a splendidly caparisoned elephant and tell the story of the Buddha. The Tooth was then taken to the temple, the people paying reverent homage as it passed. It remained in the temple for ninety days, during which time various ceremonies were performed.

Buddhadasa, who became king about the year 340, is remembered for his very great interest in medical matters. "For the good of the inhabitants of the island," state the pious authors of the *Culavamsa*, "the ruler had refuges for the sick set up in every village and placed physicians in them. He made a summary of the essential content of all the medical textbooks, and charged one physician with the care of ten villages." He is credited with a number of fabulous cures. His son "erected great nursing shelters and alms-houses for cripples, women in travail, the blind and the sick".

The fifth, sixth and seventh centuries were a time of great internal disorder and civil war. One rebel general managed to secure the help of Tamil troops from India, and these Tamils became extremely influential and powerful. During the ninth century there were further attacks from South India, and the descendants of the earlier Tamil invaders supported the Indian invaders. The island was ravaged and much booty carried away: the constant warfare sapped the energies of the people and the leaders became increasingly demoralized. Under a series of weak, inefficient, stupid, or vicious rulers, Ceylon was a tempting prey to powerful Indian princes. Early in the eleventh century the island was absorbed into the Chola Empire.

*   *   *   *   *

During this period there was no stable system of government. The king's power was absolute because he normally had at his disposal an army which he could use to suppress rivals or rebelling subjects. He was advised at court by a council of ministers, appointed by him from among the nobility. The island was divided into provinces, each under a governor who was often a member of the royal family. There was a primitive form of popular democracy in the village councils which upheld the customary law and decided questions of local importance. At first the kings were not thought to have any special divinity. They were regarded as successful chieftains who were granted sovereign powers so long as they governed justly and defended the island from foreign aggression. In later times ideas of divinity became associated with kingship, and the king demanded not only obedience and respect from his subjects, but worship as well. The crown descended from elder brother to younger brother rather than from father to eldest son.

The king sometimes took personal command of his troops, but at other times the army was under a commander-in-chief who was as often as not a member of the royal family. In return for military service the soldiers received grants of royal land: later the fact of being a tenant of royal land implied an obligation to render military service when the king demanded it.

Justice was administered by the village elders. They considered complaints from aggrieved persons and decided disputes. They had the power to punish criminals, the regulation penalties being death for murder or robbery, fines for violent assault or petty theft, and branding for cattle stealing: those who could not pay their fines had their hands cut off. "Judgments which were just," it is recorded, "were entered in books and kept in the royal palace because of the danger of miscarriages of justice."

The Buddhist monks represented an important group in the community. The king provided land for the construction of temples. The head monks were chosen by the rest of the monks from each religious community. Attached to the temples were secular officers who supervised the collection of revenue, protected and administered the temples and temple lands, and secured the food and other requirements of the monks.

The monks were in contact with Buddhist communities elsewhere, and foreign monks would visit Ceylon bringing fraternal greetings from their co-religionists. One such visitor was the Chinese, Fa Hsien, who arrived in Ceylon at the beginning of the fifth century A.D. Fa Hsien had travelled across the Gobi Desert, through Mongolia and Afghanistan, and thence to India where he spent ten years copying the Buddhist scriptures. He then travelled in a merchant ship to Ceylon where he remained two years, returning to China by way of Java.

His description of what he himself witnessed is vivid and no doubt reliable, but his hearsay reports are of doubtful authenticity. He states that Ceylon, "the land of the lion", was "a great island" to which a hundred lesser islands (presumably the Maldives) were subject. Its chief products were pearls and gems. The streets were level and well kept: at each cross-road was a Buddhist chapel. He was told that there were between 50,000 and 60,000 priests in the island. The king himself was deeply religious and played a prominent part in Buddhist cere-monial. While in Ceylon Fa Hsien obtained and copied some Buddhist scriptures in Sanskrit which were not known in China. These included a special version of the Disciplines, a new account of the origin of the universe, some important works on ecstatic contemplation, and various extracts from the sacred texts. Much of Fa Hsien's account is devoted to the religious buildings and activities which he observed. He was much impressed with the sacred Bo Tree which had been planted at Anuradhapura some seven centuries earlier and which is there to this day. It was said to have sprung from a branch of the tree under which the Buddha attained enlightenment and to have been brought to Ceylon from India during the third century B.C.

Fa Hsien tells a quaint story of how the king then ruling had one day entered the sacred treasury where the priests kept priceless gems and pearls. The sight of these costly jewels made the king envious, and he tried to carry them away forcibly. Three days later he came to his senses and returned to the treasury. There he made obeisance before the priests in re-pentance, and said to them: "I want you to make a regulation that in future no king shall be admitted to this treasury, but any religious mendicant of full forty years' standing may be allowed to enter."

The main occupation of the people was, of course, agri-culture. The climate was warm and the soil fertile. The chief

difficulty was that the rain fell during only a short period of
the year, and one of the main objects of government was to
secure adequate irrigation. This was done by building dams
across valleys and rivers, and collecting the water in reservoirs
or tanks. Great ingenuity and skill was exercised in creating a
sound system of irrigation. The labour was normally obtained
by the compulsory service of the peasants which was rendered
in lieu of rent.

There had been a certain amount of foreign trade from the
earliest times. During the eighth century Arab traders from
the Persian Gulf settled in Ceylon. They were Moslems by
religion, and their descendants in the island, known as Ceylon
Moors, comprise the majority of the Moslem community today.
They have usually engaged in trade rather than in agriculture.

Cosmas, an Egyptian traveller, writing about the middle
of the sixth century—probably from personal experience—says
that Ceylon was at that time an important commercial centre,
and trade was conducted in silk, spices and sandalwood. Ceylon,
"placed, as one may say, in the centre of the Indies . . . receives
imports from all the seats of commerce and in turn exports
to them, and is thus itself a great seat of commerce".

He reports that there was in the island a community of
Persian Christians "with clergy and a body of believers . . .
and a Presbyter who is appointed from Persia, and a Deacon
and a complete ecclesiastical ritual. But the natives and their
kings are heathens".

Cosmas relates an anecdote about a countryman of his,
Sopatrus by name, who had visited Ceylon on business. The
tale is almost certainly apocryphal since it appears in many
versions in different books, and a variant of it is recounted
by Pliny writing five centuries earlier. Sopatrus, according to
Cosmas, was in Ceylon about the same time as a ship from
Persia, and he and a Persian "of venerable age and appearance"
were taken by an official to the presence of the king. After
the usual formalities, the king asked the Persian and Sopatrus
what conditions were like in their two countries. After they
had replied the king inquired: "Which of your kings is the
greater and the more powerful?" The Persian replied: "Our
king is both the more powerful and the greater and richer,

and indeed is King of Kings, and whatsoever he desires, that
he is able to do." Sopatrus was silent, and the king asked why
he had nothing to say. Sopatrus replied that the way to learn
the truth was to examine the coins of the two kingdoms. The
king liked the idea and asked that the two coins should be
produced. The Roman coin—for Egypt was then a Roman
province—was of gold, "had a right good ring, was of bright
metal and finely shaped". The Persian coin was of silver and
much inferior. The king examined both coins carefully and
came to the conclusion that "the Romans were certainly a
splendid, powerful, and sagacious people", and he ordered great
honour to be paid to Sopatrus and caused him to be mounted
on an elephant and conducted round the city with drums
beating.

CHAPTER III

THE TAMIL INVASIONS, 1017–1505

Ripe fruit falls of itself.—Tamil proverb.

WHEN the Middle Ages dawned the part of south India known by Europeans as the Carnatic was divided into two kingdoms—Pandya and Chola. For centuries these two kingdoms had striven for mastery and had remained virtually independent of the emperors who ruled northern India. In the year 994 the Chola kingdom conquered the Pandyans, and for nearly three centuries the Chola kings were the masters of south India. Ceylon, the Malay peninsula, and the East Indies became subject to Chola rule at various times. Ceylon was conquered during the first years of the eleventh century, the Chola emperor capturing the King of Ceylon and the crown jewels in the year 1017. The island became a Chola colony and the former King of Ceylon lived in captivity in India. The royal capital Polonnaruwa was given an Indian name, and many Hindu shrines and temples were erected in different parts of the island.

At first the Cholas found that some of the descendants of the earlier Tamil immigrants and invaders would collaborate with them in administering the country; but the son of the exiled king formed a resistance movement. These rebels to Chola rule organized revolts in Ceylon itself and assisted whichever Tamil kingdoms in India happened to be at war with the Chola Empire at any particular moment. When the Chola emperor had subdued the rival kingdoms on the Indian mainland, refugees from these territories joined the resistance movement in Ceylon. These foreign supporters proved, however, to be a source of weakness rather than strength. Soon the rebels had split up into rival factions which wasted their strength on internecine struggles.

It was not until about 1055 that the unity, essential if the invading Cholas were to be ejected, was secured. The leader

26

was a youthful relative of the last king. He was a resourceful
and daring figure, "a brave man and distinguished by his good
conduct . . . extraordinarily skilled in the use of the many
expedients such as kindness . . . wise in statecraft . . . gifted
with abundant knowledge," according to the *Culavamsa*. He
knew when to attack on a broad front and when to resort to
guerrilla activity. The struggle for liberation lasted fifteen
years, and in 1070 or soon after, the prince was crowned King
of Ceylon, assuming the title of Vijayabahu I. He ruled for
forty-four years, though his reign was not a peaceful one. He
was a good king and is said to have greatly improved the
administration of justice. "He did what served the good of his
people and what at the same time was politically wise." He
had temples restored and seems to have taken a keen interest
in literature. "Himself a great poet, he gave great possessions
to many authors of poems." Royal grants were made to widows,
orphans, the blind and cripples. But ambitious generals and rival
princes intrigued to supplant him. On one occasion some Tamil
mercenaries mutinied and killed two of his generals. "After a
sharp fight he shortly put the assembled troops to flight. Placing
them around the pyre on which were laid the remains of the
murdered generals, he had the recreant leaders of the troops,
their hands bound fast to their backs, chained to a stake and
burnt in the midst of the flames blazing around them." When
he died the country fell apart into separate kingdoms.

The next king of note, Parakramabahu the Great, assumed
the throne in the year 1153. He was the grandson of the sister
of the king mentioned in the last paragraph. He was able,
ambitious and shrewd. He eliminated the various petty princes
who had seized principalities, and became sole king; but there
were constant rebellions by the princes he had deposed. He
was also involved in war with the King of Pegu in Burma,
and in the seemingly endless struggle between the rival Tamil
kingdoms in south India. He was, however, able to devote
some of his energies to peaceful pursuits. He had the irrigation
system greatly improved:

"Where there were great swamps," record the chronicles,
"he took the water and conducted it to rivers, laid out fields,

and collected a large quantity of grain. In the wilderness there and at very many other places he assembled the village chiefs and entrusted them with the cultivation of the country-side. . . . He brought it to pass that the inhabitants never knew famine. . . . He had charming parks laid out, filled with numerous kinds of creepers and trees which bore fruits and blossoms. . . . He ordered his skilled clerks to make an estimate of the royal revenues, of the stocks of grain, of the troops and war material, with the cost of each. . . . He separated the exchequer from the military department, putting each in charge of a chief official. . . . He had a great building erected for sick people. . . . To discerning and skil-ful physicians who were quick at distinguishing diseases and were versed in the medical books, he gave maintenance according to their needs."

He had Anuradhapura restored "because its soil had been hallowed by the feet of the Buddha".

He took a great interest in the building of shrines and temples. He was disgusted with the disunity in the Buddhist priesthood which had caused many priests to go and live abroad. He therefore called a conference of priests at which he presided, and was able to resolve the differences. Those who would not accept the new unity were expelled from the priesthood and given secular posts. "With great pains he established again the community as it had been in the Buddha's time." His reign has often been thought of as the period when the Sinhalese kingdom was at the zenith of its power.

*   *   *   *   *

In the twenty-eight years which followed the death of Parakramabahu in 1186, fifteen sovereigns ruled in quick suc-cession. In 1215 the throne was seized by a bigoted Hindu from south India called Magha, who persecuted the Sinhalese Buddhists, terrorized the people, and ravaged the land. "He tore from the people their garments and jewels," wrote the Buddhist chroniclers, "corrupted the good morals of family life which had been observed for ages, mutilated the people, destroyed many houses, and captured oxen and cattle. They put fetters on the wealthy and made poor people of them. They desecrated the temples, ill-treated the priests, flogged the children, and destroyed the sacred books." According to the *Rajavaliya*, Magha "wrought confusion in castes by reducing to servitude people of high birth in Ceylon, raising people of low birth and holding them in high esteem".

Ceylon during this period was under constant foreign attack. Improvements in ship construction had made it easier for Asian monarchs to establish empires by subjugating and absorbing small neighbours. At various times in the thirteenth, fourteenth, and fifteenth centuries, Ceylon was subordinate to the various south Indian kingdoms; the Emperor of China; a Malayan king; and possibly for short periods to the King of Pegu in Burma and to the Sultan of Egypt.

In addition Ceylon was receiving the attention of European visitors. Most occidental travellers to China and the Far East made Ceylon a port of call.

From this time Ceylon was usually divided into two kingdoms. In the region of Jaffna in the north was a Tamil kingdom which as often as not accepted the suzerainty of one of the Hindu empires in south India. The Sinhalese kings were driven more and more to the south-west. Eventually Polonnaruwa was abandoned as a capital, and when the Portuguese arrived at the beginning of the sixteenth century, the Sinhalese capital was at Kotte, a few miles from Colombo.

Occasionally a Sinhalese king would regain some of the northern territory. Parakramabahu II, who reigned from about 1235 to 1270, recaptured Polonnaruwa in 1244. He might have been successful in conquering the whole of the north but for the fact that a few months later Ceylon was invaded by a Malay king and for some time his martial energies were devoted to ejecting this invader and his mercenaries. Parakramabahu II was at heart a scholar rather than a soldier. He was called by his contemporaries "The-scholar-who-is-entirely-familiar-with-the-literature-of-the-present-era". He was much interested in religious matters and tried to improve the discipline of the Buddhist priesthood.

After the death of Parakramabahu II there was a period of

some thirty years of disorder and anarchy. There was an invasion from India in the 1270s which led the Sinhalese kings
to look for foreign allies. An embassy proposing an alliance was
sent to Egypt in 1283. Chinese ambassadors probably visited
various kingdoms in South-East Asia about this time. In 1281,
according to Marco Polo, a Chinese embassy arrived in Ceylon.
Kublai Khan had apparently heard from some Arabs that
certain of the Buddha's sacred relics were in Ceylon. He sent
an embassy to the King of Ceylon asking that he might have
them. The king gave the ambassadors "two large back teeth,
together with some of the hair, and a handsome vessel". When
the Great Khan heard of the success of the embassy, he ordered
all the people of his capital to march out of the city to meet
the ambassadors, and they were conducted to his presence with
great pomp and solemnity.

Marco Polo had visited Ceylon, probably about the year
1294, on his way home to Europe after his seventeen years of
service with Kublai Khan. Ceylon was in a state of confusion
and turmoil at the time. Troops from south India had carried
off the Tooth Relic, and since the death of the younger son of
Parakramabahu II, no Sinhalese king had defied the invaders
from across the straits. Marco Polo says that Ceylon was
"independent of every other state" and he gives the name of
the king who was reigning at the time. The name is almost
certainly an Indian one and there is little doubt that he was in
fact the Pandyan governor of the island.

Though Marco Polo did not stay long, he was much impressed with the island. "For its size," he remarks, "it is better
circumstanced than any other island in the world." The people,
both men and women, went about almost unclothed, "only wrap-
ping a cloth round the middle part of their bodies". The main
crops were sesame, from which oil was expressed, and rice. The
people ate rice and meat, and drank milk and coco-nut wine.

In 1302 the grandson of Parakramabahu II seems to have
decided to bow to the inevitable and accept Pandyan suzerainty.
"As he saw no other means but friendly negotiation, he set
forth for the Pandyan kingdom in the company of several able
warriors and sought out the Pandyan ruler. By daily conversa-
tions he inclined him favourably, and received from his hands

the Tooth Relic." But the Pandyan kingdom was itself doomed and succumbed a few years later to the rising power of the Moslems in India. The Sinhalese once again established themselves in the south of Ceylon, while the Tamil kingdom of Jaffna in the north remained independent.

Some years after the return of Marco Polo, the Franciscan Friar Odoric was dispatched on a missionary journey to the East. Odoric, a saintly ascetic, passed through Ceylon about the year 1321 on his journey to China. He describes the animals he found:

"an infinite number of serpents, and great store of lions, bears, and all kinds of raving wild beasts, and especially elephants. . . . The people told me that these beasts would not invade nor hurt any stranger, but only the natural inhabitants. I saw in this island fowls as big as our country geese having two heads [perhaps the rhinoceros hornbill, a bird with two bills] and other miraculous things which I will not write of here."

Like most other visitors to Ceylon the friar was impressed by the beautiful gems. "These precious stones the king takes not for his own use but once or twice every year he permits certain poor people to dive under the water for the stones, and all that they can get he bestows upon them, to the end that they may pray for his soul. . . ."

Another visitor to Ceylon about this time was John of Marignolli, Papal Legate to the Court of the Great Khan, who was detained for four months by a tyrannical chief who confiscated a great deal of treasure that he was taking to the Pope from the Great Khan and other princes. He was impressed with the piety of the Buddhist monks who were strict vegetarians and were naked except for a simple loin cloth. Their fragile houses were constructed of palm leaves.

Ibn Battuta, one of the greatest Moslem travellers of all times, visited Ceylon in 1344. He was a Moroccan who for thirty years wandered about Asia and Africa, covering some 75,000 miles in all. Unfortunately he kept no detailed record of his travels and the few notes which he had were stolen from

him, but when he returned home he dictated his memoirs to
a secretary in the Sultan's court.

He visited Puttalam, "a small pretty town, surrounded by
a wooden wall with wooden towers," which was in the Tamil
kingdom in the north of Ceylon. The sailors told him that
the ruler of this kingdom was "an evil tyrant and keeps pirate
vessels", but he was received in a friendly manner and the
ruler told him that he and his companions had permission to
land and were to be his guests. He enjoyed "great consideration
which increased every day" and had several interviews with
the ruler, who spoke Persian. One day, after presenting Ibn
Battuta with some pearls, the ruler said to him: "Do not be
reticent, but ask me for anything that you want." Ibn Battuta
replied that his one desire was to visit Adam's Peak. To this
request the ruler agreed, and a few days later Ibn Battuta set
off with an escort of slaves, priests, and court officials.

Ibn Battuta had seen Adam's Peak in the distance soon
after leaving India, "rising into the heavens like a column of
smoke". He climbed to the summit with the help of the iron
chains which are still in use to this day. He examined the footprint which he believed to be Adam's; and he described how
the priests would scramble to possess the offerings of gems left
by pious pilgrims.

Ibn Battuta was impressed by the tolerance of the Sinhalese
to non-Buddhists, and contrasts this attitude with the rigid caste
restrictions which he encountered among the Hindus of India.
The Sinhalese Buddhists were, of course, idolaters and infidels
in his view, but he says that they "show respect for Moslem
priests, lodge them in their houses, and give them to eat . . .
and have no suspicions regarding their dealings with the wives
and children".

In the course of his travels in Ceylon, Ibn Battuta visited
Chilaw, Dondra, Kurunegala, Galle, and Colombo. At Dondra
he visited the magnificent temple which the Portuguese wantonly
destroyed two and a half centuries later. Colombo was then
"one of the finest and largest towns in Ceylon". The chief
official there, records Ibn Battuta, had in his suite 500
Ethiopians, presumably slaves or mercenaries.

*   *   *   *   *

The existence of two kingdoms, a Tamil one in the north and a Sinhalese one in the south, emphasized and exaggerated the differences of language and religion between the two communities that had arrived in Ceylon from India at different times in the past. Down to our own times these differences had formed an obstacle to political progress.

The Tamil kingdom reached the height of its power in the second half of the fourteenth century. Several attempts to conquer the Sinhalese in the south were almost successful. By 1385, however, the Tamil kingdom in the north had become subject to one of the south Indian kingdoms and for a century made no show of independence.

In the Low Country a succession of Sinhalese sovereigns of little note maintained a precarious independence. In 1410, however, the royal family was captured by a Chinese ambassador and carried off to China. For half a century Ceylon was a vassal of the Chinese emperor. This period of Chinese overlordship was largely nominal, however, and a great Sinhalese king rose to supremacy. Parakramabahu VI succeeded to the throne shortly after the capture of the royal family by the Chinese, and he ruled until 1467 from his capital at Kotte. "He was dowered with faith, discernment and charity," records the *Culavamsa*, "a superb jewel of virtue, recognizing the worthlessness of acquired riches, unwearied in wise and meritorious works". He conquered the northern Tamil kingdom and repelled an invasion from India. His long reign was notable for a great cultural revival. Ceylon was raised to a height it had not known for two centuries.

After the reign of Parakramabahu VI, another period of disorder ensued. The Tamil kingdom at Jaffna again asserted its independence. Rebellions were frequent, and Kandy fell into the hands of turbulent chiefs. When the sixteenth century dawned Ceylon was like a ripe fruit waiting to be plucked by the first predatory passer-by.

*   *   *   *   *

Let us now consider the sort of society that existed during these five centuries. In the political and administrative sphere

c

we find that in spite of the difficulties caused by civil war and
foreign invasion there was a growing efficiency. Hitherto there
had been a good deal of flexibility in government. Law was
little more than the king's personal interpretation of ancient
custom. This was still true in large measure, but there was a
growing rigidity in the affairs of state. The king's council no
longer consisted solely of his personal friends. Traditions had
grown up which decreed its membership. "If the king be a
man of great abilities," stated a Kandyan priest, "well skilled
in ancient laws and usages, acquainted with the practices of
former kings, and properly versed in religious knowledge, there
are some matters which he may decide according to his own
pleasure; but there are, likewise, many others which he cannot
determine without consulting the ministers and the people."

The division of the country into provinces and counties no
longer depended on the whims of a prince or general to the
extent that it had previously. Departments of State were
created, and there was a certain continuity of officials and
policy in spite of changes of personnel at the top.

The king's council usually consisted of the heir to the throne,
the other royal princes, the officials of the royal household, the
commander-in-chief of the army, the provincial governors, and
the superintendents of the counties, together with representatives of the nobility and a number of leading merchants. There
was a growing tendency to associate ideas of divinity with kingship. The monarch was regarded as a personification of deity.

Although the kings were thought to possess divine attributes,
the pious Buddhist chroniclers did not hesitate to note royal
failures to live up to high standards.

"In their heedless way of acting," they wrote of certain
kings, "they slighted people of good family and placed
ambitious men of the lower classes in leading positions. . . .
In their insatiability and lust for money they crushed the
people by levying excessive taxes, as sugar cane is crushed in
a sugar mill. . . . The slaves and respectable artisans despised
their masters. . . . They became royal mercenaries, worming
their way into the confidence of royalty, and by securing
positions of importance exercised great power. . . . The

rulers forsook the path of good and ancient custom: they were lacking in dignity, their minds bent on destruction, deficient in royal pride, false to their own welfare and that of others, lacking in restraint."

Although in times of peace there was some foreign trade, most of the island's commerce was internal. The mass of the people grew their own food, built their own homes and furniture, and made their own clothes. In remote parts trade was carried on by barter. Coins had, however, been introduced as early as A.D. 1000; and the value of the metals used to mint the coinage varied from period to period and is some indication of the degree of prosperity which prevailed at different times.

The main foreign trade was in cinnamon, precious stones, and elephants. Cinnamon was a government monopoly—a system continued by the European conquerors. It grew wild, and the work of peeling was the compulsory service of a special caste who, in return, received grants of land. Ceylon has always been famous for its gems and, as we have noticed already, emperors as far afield as China sent to Ceylon when they wanted to improve the crown jewels.

A complicated system of land tenure was growing up. Peasants who occupied land rendered certain services in lieu of rent. In some areas there was a tax of about one-tenth of the annual produce which went into the royal coffers. Death duties were also paid. Forced labour was used to maintain roads, paths, and bridges, and in addition certain services for the upkeep of temples and the estates of the nobility were required.

Local militia were conscripted for the purpose of carrying on the wars, and in addition foreign mercenaries were frequently employed. Weapons were comparatively primitive and warfare was normally of a guerrilla nature.

The king and nobility, and indeed the common people, took their religious duties very seriously. The ascribing of divine attributes to the monarch symbolized the close connection between church and state. Many of the kings were very devout men who encouraged the construction of temples and shrines. Ceylon, indeed, had its reformations. Heretical Budd-

hist sects frequently sprang up, and there were occasional
schisms within the priesthood.

Hinduism, like Buddhism, is a gentle and tolerant religion,
but some of the Tamil conquerors were violent in their per-
secution of the Buddhist religion. Shrines and temples were
destroyed and their wealth looted.

One important consequence of the presence of the Hindu
and Buddhist religions side by side was the permeation of
Buddhism with the caste system. Caste was originally a Hindu
institution: the word caste itself is believed to be derived from
a Portuguese word meaning colour. When the early Aryan
invaders arrived in India they were paler in colour than the
people they conquered. It seems that at first a person's caste
was determined by the quantity of Aryan blood in his veins,
but later the distinction became occupational as well as racial.
A caste was a Hindu social group, membership of which was
decided by birth. An orthodox Hindu could not change from
one caste to another, could not marry a person from another
caste, could not eat or mingle socially with a person from
another caste. At first there were only four castes—priests,
warriors, merchants and craftsmen, and labourers. Gradually
new caste distinctions were recognized. This Hindu system
was introduced to Ceylon by the Tamils and was adopted by
the Buddhist population. In the process, however, it became a
less rigid institution than it had been on the Indian mainland,
and during the nineteenth and twentieth centuries it began to
break down under the impact of western ideas. In other ways,
too, Hinduism and Buddhism intermingled. Hindu deities were
often worshipped in Buddhist temples.

As in most countries of the world at this period, art and
literature was closely associated with religion. This was mainly
because the priests were the only people with the time and
training to devote themselves to literary pursuits. The com-
pilation of chronicles and epic poems was a religious duty. It
was inevitable that, as elsewhere, cultural diversions were confined to the few, and the mass of the people remained ignorant,
illiterate, and superstitious.

CHAPTER IV

THE PORTUGUESE PERIOD, 1505-1658

He who breaks a bee-hive will soon lick his hand.—
Sinhalese proverb.

THE inspiring words about England which Shakespeare put into the mouth of John of Gaunt have already been quoted. John's daughter Philippa married King John I of Portugal, and their son attained renown as Prince Henry the Navigator. Portugal, under Prince Henry's leadership, became the greatest maritime nation in the world. The Cape route to the East was discovered soon after Henry's death, and in 1498 Vasco da Gama reached Calicut in India. Seven years later a Portuguese fleet, apparently driven off course in a gale, anchored off Colombo. The captain of the Portuguese ships asked if he could discuss trade matters with the king, and a Portuguese representative was conducted to Kotte, about six miles from Colombo. This journey took three days—an effort on the part of the Sinhalese to give the foreigner the impression that here was a vast empire. News of the Portuguese was sent from Colombo to the court by a less circuitous way. "There is in our harbour of Colombo a race of people fair of skin and comely withal. They don jackets of iron and hats of iron: they rest not a minute in one place: they walk here and there. . . . The report of their cannon is louder than thunder."

When the Portuguese representative reached the court he was taken to the presence of the king and his ministers, and there announced that his nation desired to trade. The king and the ministers readily agreed to the Portuguese proposal, and a treaty was concluded providing that the Portuguese might trade in cinnamon, in return for which they would defend the seaboard of Ceylon from attack. The Portuguese were given permission to engrave the royal arms on a boulder overlooking Colombo. The memorial can still be seen, although it inexplicably has the date 1501 engraved beside it.

The era of Portuguese supremacy in Ceylon can be con-
sidered in two distinct periods. The first period corresponded
approximately to the sixteenth century. During this time the
Portuguese were at the height of their power throughout the
East. In 1500 the Portuguese King Emanuel had assumed the
title of "Lord of the Conquest, Navigation and Commerce of
India, Ethiopia, Arabia, and Persia", a title confirmed by Pope
Alexander VI in 1502. Portuguese trading stations were estab-
lished in India, the Malay peninsula, and the East Indies, and
China and Japan were opened to foreign trade. So far as
Ceylon was concerned, the record is one of steadily increasing
Portuguese control. There were setbacks, it is true, but the
general trend is clear. By the turn of the century Ceylon had
passed under formal Portuguese sovereignty.

The second period, corresponding approximately to the first
half of the seventeenth century, was one of Portuguese decline.
The causes of the decline are complex and outside the scope
of this book. Towards the end of the sixteenth century Portugal
had come under the sway of Spain and as a consequence became
involved in war with the Netherlands. The Dutch gradually
replaced the Portuguese as the great maritime nation of the
East.

The Portuguese were interested in Ceylon not only because
of its wealth of spices and gems but because of its strategic
position in the Indian Ocean. If they were to be masters of the
Orient they could not afford to allow Ceylon to remain independent or to fall into hostile hands. Time and again they were
almost driven from the island, but their control of the sea
enabled them to send reinforcements from India and restore
their position. So long as they were opposed by native kings
or princes they were secure. It was the presence of a skilful
European rival, with its own navy, that finally led to the
downfall of the Portuguese.

The Portuguese strategy was not original. They offered to
defend native kingdoms from external attack in exchange for
trading privileges and the right to erect forts and establish
garrisons. *Divide et impera* is an old maxim. In the unscrupulous
hands of the Portuguese this policy was brought to a fine art.
If a native protégé became too powerful, they unhesitatingly

transferred their support to a rival. They plotted and intrigued. Their officials were greedy and corrupt. Though they paid lip-service to the Christian religion and though a number of officials and missionaries were devoted servants of the Gospel, the general record is one of ruthless and rapacious conquest. One Sinhalese who was given a copy of the New Testament by a Jesuit missionary returned a few months later in bewilderment. Jesus Christ, he said, had never taken money from anyone. Why were the Portuguese Christians so grasping?

There is no more forceful indictment of Portuguese policy and practice in Ceylon than that of one of their own country-men, Father Fernão de Queyroz, a Jesuit priest who lived in India during the latter period of the Portuguese occupation. "We could have been masters of India," he wrote, "if we had been masters of ourselves." His detailed history of the Portuguese conquest of Ceylon was written to show that the physical subjugation of the country was futile unless its inhabitants were conquered spiritually. He thought that the behaviour of the Portuguese in Ceylon explained why the people of the island retained their non-Christian beliefs. "We have no reason to be surprised at the heavy punishment which God there inflicted on the Portuguese nation, her enemies increasing in proportion as the guilt increased, till finally the whole island was lost and God gave over to unbelievers and heretics what Catholic Christians did not deserve to keep." His condemnation of Portuguese rule was precise and fully documented. Page after page is filled with examples of cruelties and atrocities too horrible, almost, to be believed.

The Sinhalese were by nature a gentle and pacific people. Father Queyroz described them as "extremely gentle by nature", and Marco Polo wrote that they were "by no means of a military habit, but . . . abject and timid; and when there is occasion to employ soldiers, they are procured from other countries". Buddhism, like Christianity, is a religion of kindliness and pity. The Sinhalese were shocked at the arrogance and cruelty of their European conquerors.

*   *   *   *   *

The Portuguese left a few officials at Colombo to superintend future trade after their chance visit in 1505. For a time their contact with Ceylon was perfunctory, mainly because their energies became absorbed in the more pressing conflict with Egypt. In 1517, however, a Portuguese fleet anchored off Colombo. This time it was not a fortuitous visit, but part of a planned campaign.

The Portuguese governor was taken into the presence of the Sinhalese king. There he declared the implacable hatred of the Portuguese for the Moslem religion. It was this hatred, he said, which had brought the Portuguese to the East and to fulfil their purpose it was necessary to build a fort in Colombo and man it with Portuguese troops. He added that the king would be well advised to drive the Moors (Arabs) from his realm. The king asked that he might have two days to consult his noblemen about the matter.

While the king and his councillors deliberated, riots broke out in Colombo. The Portuguese governor landed some troops, set fire to the town, and began to build a fort. He then sent a message to the king saying that "unless he wished to see his lands destroyed . . . he must become a tributary to the King of Portugal". The king accepted the Portuguese terms and the governor departed. A small Portuguese garrison was left in Colombo.

The Portuguese were quick to exploit internal differences and dynastic rivalries. In 1521 the Sinhalese king died, leaving three princes born to the woman who had been consort to him and his brother. The eldest prince succeeded to the throne. "This king was beloved of all," wrote a Portuguese priest, "for as he was affable, he was esteemed by those who knew how to value this quality, and few feared his rigour. He was liberal to excess, more a friend of peace than of war, for he was by nature gentle. Of his own interest he was negligent, but not so of public affairs . . . gay in conversation, acute and piquant in speech, but truthful in his dealings". The Sinhalese chroniclers were less sympathetic: they wrote that "he lived foolishly on terms of close intimacy with the Portuguese. . . . He did harm to the religion of the illustrious Ceylon—harm which will last for years to come".

In order to placate his brothers he created two principalities in different parts of his kingdom, and each brother was put in charge of one of these. Quarrels soon broke out. One of the brothers, Mayadunne, was an ambitious young man who wished to supplant his brother as king. "He even intended," wrote Father Queyroz, "to become lord of the whole kingdom and aspired to the dominion of the whole island." Having consolidated his position in his own principality with its capital at Sitawaka, Mayadunne attacked his brother. He sought and obtained the assistance of the ruler of Calicut in India, and the Sinhalese king therefore turned to the Portuguese who had promised to defend his kingdom. The effect of this internecine warfare was merely to weaken Ceylon and strengthen the Portuguese.

The first phase of the struggle between Mayadunne and his Indian allies on the one hand and the king and his Portuguese allies on the other lasted nearly twenty years. Several times the king's capital at Kotte was blockaded by Mayadunne and only saved by the arrival of reinforcements from Goa, the Portuguese headquarters in India. The climax came in 1538 when Mayadunne's Indian allies were heavily defeated by the Portuguese in a naval engagement near the island of Rameswaram.

The Portuguese had no reason to regret the rivalry between the king and his brother Mayadunne. Though they always honoured their treaty with the king or gave a plausible explanation of their failure to do so, they contrived to keep the family quarrel in being.

The king had only one child, a daughter, by his principal queen, and Mayadunne hoped that even if he could not seize the throne by force, he would succeed to the kingdom in the event of his brother's death. Such a prospect was most displeasing to the Portuguese. "Since it seemed more in the interests of Your Highness that the island should not belong to one alone, but to several," wrote the Portuguese Viceroy to his sovereign, "former governors did not interfere in this matter and left them to go on with their quarrels." The Portuguese were determined that the king should not nominate Mayadunne as his successor. Eventually the king was persuaded to nominate

as his successor his grandson Dharmapala. A gorgeous cere-
mony was held in Portugal in which the succession to Dharmapala was confirmed. The former treaty between the Portuguese
and the Sinhalese was elaborated, and the king agreed to the
dispatch of six Christian missionaries to Ceylon.

About the same time an Indian convert of Francis Xavier
arrived in the island. Large numbers of Sinhalese embraced
the Christian faith. The energy, zeal and fanaticism of the
Portuguese in their efforts to secure converts is well known.

"We charge you," wrote the King of Portugal to his
Viceroy in the East, "to discover all the idols by means of
diligent officers, to reduce them to fragments and utterly
consume them. . . . And because the heathen submit themselves to the yoke of the Gospel not alone through the
conviction of the purity of the Faith and for that they are
sustained by the hope of Eternal Life, they should also be
encouraged with some temporal favours. . . . And, therefore,
you should earnestly set yourself to see that the new
Christians from this time forward do obtain and enjoy all
exemptions and freedom from tribute."

Determined efforts were made to convert the Sinhalese king:
"if the king became a Christian, that would be sufficient for
all to become the same". One Portuguese military commander
who had been describing to the king the torments of hell was
astonished when the anxious king asked if he had himself
experienced them. "Many low-caste people," recorded the
chroniclers, "intermarried with the Portuguese and became
proselytes."

Meanwhile Mayadunne and the Portuguese had been in
secret communication. Mayadunne suggested to the Portuguese
that his royal brother was insincere in his apparent friendship
for Portugal and that he was in reality plotting to kill all the
Portuguese in the island. The Portuguese, anxious to test the
king's loyalty in the light of Mayadunne's accusations, asked
the king for concrete evidence of his friendship in the shape
of a series of lavish presents for the Viceroy. The king realized
that his reputation was dwindling and complied with this

request. A few months later he was murdered by his guard who was probably in the pay of the Portuguese. "Some say that this hurt was done of set purpose," wrote a chronicler in the *Rajavaliya*, "others that it was done unwittingly: God alone knoweth which is true."

Young Dharmapala, the dead king's grandson, now succeeded to the throne in accordance with the arrangements made a decade before. As he was a minor, his father acted as regent. There was great resentment on the part of the Sinhalese at the murder of the king, and the Portuguese hurriedly departed from Colombo. The Portuguese Viceroy immediately organized an expedition to restore his damaged fortunes. A large army arrived at Colombo, occupied the capital, arrested the royal officials, ransacked the palace, and seized everything of value. A temporary agreement with Dharmapala was, however, fixed up, and a joint Portuguese-Sinhalese army set off to subjugate Mayadunne. Dharmapala had to pay the expenses of the expedition, and to do this was compelled to sell the crown jewels. When the Portuguese troops arrived at Mayadunne's capital they found it deserted. The city was sacked and the royal palace destroyed. The Portuguese Viceroy then sent a message to Dharmapala urging him to accept the Christian faith.

The behaviour of the Portuguese during this period was particularly shameful. No attempt was made to prevent the soldiery from looting. Women were openly raped, temples wantonly desecrated, young children sold into slavery.

The Portuguese now felt that Dharmapala had been sufficiently weakened and decided that Mayadunne, who controlled much of the interior of the island, must be bought or conquered. Portuguese agents again got in touch with him and offered to make him king under their protection if he would help in eliminating Dharmapala and the court at Kotte. For a time Mayadunne seems to have toyed with the idea of co-operating with the Portuguese. There was confused fighting in which the Portuguese seem to have assisted Mayadunne in attacking the regent. Mayadunne's troops were commanded by his son, said by some Sinhalese chroniclers to have been only twelve years old at the time. For his exploits in the field of battle he was granted the title of Rajasinha, the Lion King.

Dharmapala was by now a mere puppet of the Portuguese. In 1557 he and his consort were baptized into the Christian Church: they took the names of Don John and Dona Catherina, after the Portuguese sovereigns. This was a great triumph for the Portuguese, but it alienated the king still further from his subjects. "This kingdom," wrote a contemporary Sinhalese historian, "can never be governed by a king who is not of the religion of Buddha."

Mayadunne seized the opportunity to present himself to the people of Ceylon as their saviour. He appealed to what we would now call their nationalist sentiments. The king at Kotte had been installed under Portuguese protection, had accepted the Portuguese religion, was advised by Portuguese officials. All who cared for indigenous traditions and culture should rally to the standard of Mayadunne.

The Portuguese supported the declining power of Dharmapala and the Sinhalese dynasty at Kotte, but in spite of this Mayadunne steadily increased his control. In 1565 Dharmapala abandoned his capital and took refuge in the Portuguese fort at Colombo. The ancient Sinhalese kingdom which, under various dynasties, had survived for over 2,000 years was almost at an end.

The forces of Mayadunne's kingdom of Sitawaka were now commanded by his son Rajasinha, who harried and chased the Portuguese almost at will. In 1578 Mayadunne, who was more than eighty years old, abdicated in favour of Rajasinha. Rajasinha immediately proceeded to invest Colombo, and for nearly two years the town was blockaded. The siege was only ended by the arrival of Portuguese reinforcements. The cruelty of the Portuguese on this occasion almost beggars description. One Portuguese official describes how a Sinhalese soldier who had killed twenty-nine Portuguese levies was captured and taken to Colombo. Here a Portuguese soldier killed him in cold blood, cut open the heart, and drank the dead man's blood. When Mayadunne died in 1581 Rajasinha was master of all of Ceylon except for Colombo and its environs, and a small area in the north. Dharmapala, a tool of the Portuguese, executed an instrument appointing King Philip of Portugal as his legal heir.

Rajasinha was determined to drive the hated Portuguese out of the country and establish himself on the throne of his fathers. The whole island was mobilized for a desperate onslaught on Colombo. An army estimated at between 50,000 and 60,000 men reached the outskirts of the city in 1587. The attempt to capture the fort was in vain but Colombo was besieged. For a time it seemed as if the siege might be successful, but command of the sea once again enabled the Portuguese to send reinforcements from India. Rajasinha withdrew and the Portuguese began an orgy of plunder and wanton destruction. The sacred temples at Dondra were ransacked and then destroyed.

Rajasinha was exhausted by the struggle, and a period of truce ensued. In 1593 he died of blood poisoning from a bamboo splinter. "Verily this sinner did rule with a strong arm," commented a Buddhist chronicler. To this day he remains a hero to the Sinhalese. He was the last native king to defy the encroaching Europeans.

Rajasinha's grandson succeeded to the throne, but he was assassinated the following year. The Sitawaka kingdom now collapsed. One of the ablest generals deserted to the aging Dharmapala who still lived at Kotte as a pathetic Portuguese puppet. The kingdom of Sitawaka, which had been ruled over first by Mayadunne and then by Rajasinha, ceased to exist, and for a few brief years the unfortunate Dharmapala controlled most of the kingdom which had come to him from his grandfather.

It was at this point that the Portuguese decided on a change of policy. Hitherto their intervention in the affairs of Ceylon had been in defence of the Sinhalese monarch. He was now an old man, "the figure rather than the reality of a king," as a Portuguese historian expressed it, and he had arranged that his kingdom should pass into Portuguese hands on his death. The only obstacle to absolute Portuguese control of the island was the semi-independent kingdom of Kandy in the interior. The Portuguese resolved to capture this kingdom by force of arms. A Captain-General of the Conquest was appointed and arrived in Ceylon with a Portuguese army. He was joined by a collection of regular Sinhalese soldiers, mercenaries, and bandits, and the advance on Kandy began. They found the territory deserted and placed on the throne a Sinhalese princess whom they thought would be loyal to them. They planned that she should marry a Portuguese nobleman, who, says Father Quey-roz, "was the strongest and most shapely of all the Portuguese. . . . But he, like a prudent man, refused the honour." This was, however, only a mild setback compared with what was to follow. The Portuguese Captain-General quarrelled with the senior native commander and killed him. At this point the King of Kandy counter-attacked. The Portuguese were cut to pieces, and the princess they had intended for the Kandyan throne fell into the hands of the Kandyan king, who promptly married her.

In 1597 Dharmapala's pathetic life came to an end and King Philip of Portugal became the legal sovereign of Ceylon. Sinhalese representatives gathered at Malwana and took the oath of allegiance to the new European king. The first phase of the Portuguese era in Ceylon was at an end.

* * * * *

It was during the year in which the Portuguese succeeded to the formal sovereignty over Ceylon that another event took place which was to be of great significance to the future of the island. In 1597 the Dutch established a trading station in Java: five years later Dutch ships appeared off the east coast of Ceylon and proceeded to the Kandyan court. The Dutch made a good impression on the king and a few months later another party visited the court.

The Dutch, of course, were intent on destroying the Portuguese monopoly of the trade of the Orient, and in their struggle for supremacy they welcomed all allies. The Kandyan kingdom was at war with the Portuguese, therefore the Kandyan kingdom should be supported. "No place would be better for attacking the Portuguese," wrote a Dutch official, "if only we can keep the king and the people of the country our friends."

Meanwhile the Kandyan armies were steadily extending their control of the island. Some of the Portuguese levies deserted to the Kandyans, and it seemed as if the Portuguese might be driven from Ceylon. It was at this critical juncture that the Dutch fleet arrived at Batticaloa on the east coast. The Kandyan king went on board a ship to discuss with the Dutch concerted plans to get rid of the Portuguese. Evidence as to what exactly happened next is conflicting. The Dutch admiral was drunk and apparently insulted the king: there was some sort of brawl in which the admiral was killed. The king, who was not present when this happened, became panic-stricken and decided that his safest course was to massacre those of the Dutch who were on shore. When the news of this reached the Dutch ships, a message was sent to the king demanding an explanation. "He who drinks wine is vile," replied the king curtly. "God has wrought justice. If you desire peace, it is peace. If war, war." The Dutch fleet departed in haste.

The following year the king died. His son was a minor so he was succeeded as sovereign by his cousin Senarat, who until that time had been a priest. Senarat determined to repair the damage done by the late king's quarrel with the Dutch. In 1612 a treaty was signed in which he and the Dutch agreed to co-operate in fighting the Portuguese: the Dutch were given permission to build a fort at Cottiar on the east coast and were granted a monopoly of the trade in cinnamon, gems and pearls: two Dutch advisers were included in the Sinhalese war council. The Dutch were granted extraterritorial rights.

The Portuguese, unable to defeat the Kandyans in open battle, adopted new tactics. Twice a year a party of Portuguese troops and levies would proceed to the interior on a campaign of plunder. The countryside would be ravaged, adult males killed, the women sent to brothels, the children sold into slavery, the cattle seized. It was symptomatic of the decadence of the Portuguese Empire that they had no policy except brigandage and piracy.

This continued for some years, and was followed by an uneasy period of truce. In 1629, however, hostilities broke out again. Once more the Portuguese, with 13,000 native levies, passed through the countryside on their destructive errand. Their army was surrounded and virtually annihilated. When the head of the Portuguese general was brought to Senarat, he

commented sadly: "How often did I ask you not to make war
on me, nor destroy my lands, but to let me live in peace, while
you Portuguese remained absolute lords of the best part of
Ceylon: but if your successors follow in your footsteps, you
will not be the last."

A month later the Kandyan troops reached the outskirts
of Colombo and for three months the town was beseiged.
When Portuguese reinforcements arrived, the Kandyans withdrew. Further Portuguese reinforcements arrived from India
the following year and Senarat again agreed to a truce.

Senarat died in 1635 and was succeeded by his youngest
son, who had been *de facto* ruler for some years: he took the
title Rajasinha II. An Englishman who knew Rajasinha well
wrote that he was "an absolute tyrant, and rules the most
arbitrarily of any king in the world . . . crafty, cautious, a great
dissembler . . . naturally disposed to cruelty". He had "great
rolling eyes . . . a brisk bold look, a great swelling belly . . .
somewhat bald". The Buddhist chroniclers say that he was "a
man whose commands were not lightly to be disregarded,
difficult to attack, hard to vanquish, of a lion-like courage . . .
pious in the faith".

Soon the Portuguese were at war with the Kandyans again.
Rajasinha sent a message asking why the Portuguese insisted
on making war. He had paid his tribute regularly, he said, and
he was at a loss to understand the reason for the Portuguese
attack. One of the Portuguese officers merely commented: "The
little black is frightened. We will drag him out by the ears."
The Portuguese advanced to the Kandyan capital, finding it
deserted, but on their return they were surrounded and mas-
sacred. Of an army of 900 Portuguese only thirty-three survived.

Rajasinha now communicated with the Dutch, declaring
himself "a brother in war to the king of the Hollanders as long
as the sun and moon shall continue in the firmament", and
assuring the Dutch that they could build a fort at Cottiar or
Batticaloa. The Dutch replied by offering to supply Rajasinha
with arms in exchange for some cinnamon. The Dutch letter
concluded: "We acknowledge we ought to have presented your
majesty with some foreign rarities, according to custom. But
being ignorant of the condition of your country and in no

small fear that our envoys might be detained by the Portuguese, we hope your majesty will excuse the same for this time." Rajasinha suggested a more active partnership than the Dutch had proposed. He would attack Colombo if the Dutch would render naval assistance. The Dutch agreed to this course. The Portuguese were now in a hopeless position. Batticaloa was captured in 1638, Trincomalee in 1639, Negombo and Galle in 1640. Meanwhile a formal treaty had been signed between Rajasinha and the Dutch. This provided for joint action against the Portuguese—the full cost being paid by Rajasinha—and a Dutch monopoly of Ceylon's external trade. The third article of the treaty gave rise to a good deal of trouble later: it appears to have been included in certain copies of the treaty and omitted from others:

> "After the taking of any forts, the Dutch shall provide the same with necessary garrisons and ammunition; and if anything be wanted to complete the fortifications, the same shall be done at the charge of his majesty as it shall be thought requisite by the Dutch."

The Kandyans and the Dutch co-operated while the struggle was at its height, but as victory came in sight disagreements about petty details became more frequent. Rajasinha was glad of Dutch help in getting rid of the hated Portuguese. Whether he thought further ahead than that is doubtful. Certain it is that the Dutch were determined to stay in Ceylon. The Dutch commander went to the court of Rajasinha to discuss the grievances. The interview was cold and formal. On his way home he insulted his native escort, and was murdered.

The breach between Rajasinha and the Dutch enabled the Portuguese to restore their lost fortunes, and shortly afterwards formal peace was concluded between the Dutch and Portuguese nations. The consequence, so far as Ceylon was concerned, was to partition the island into Dutch and Portuguese spheres of influence, though Rajasinha did his best to set the two intruding European nations at odds.

War between the Portuguese and the Dutch broke out again in 1652. For some time the Portuguese were able to maintain

D

their position, even to attack, but in 1655 Dutch reinforcements
arrived. The Portuguese fought bravely against tremendous
odds. After a siege lasting six months the Portuguese at Colombo
capitulated. It was an irony of fate that Rajasinha was prevented
by an attack of fever from sharing in the final overthrow of the
Portuguese.

*   *   *   *   *

The period of Portuguese supremacy in Ceylon had lasted
a century and a half. Their record of colonial administration
must, of course, be considered against the standards prevailing
at the time. Sir Emerson Tenn nt wrote that "there is no page
in the story of European colonization more gloomy and repul-
sive than that which recounts the proceedings of the Portuguese
in Ceylon". Their conduct, he said, was characterized by
"rapacity, bigotry and cruelty". Though harsh, this judgment
is not unmerited. On the other hand, something can be said in
defence of the Portuguese.

Conditions in Ceylon were bad when they arrived. Although
a king nominally ruled from his capital at Kotte, his actual
control of the island was extremely limited. External trade was
largely in the hands of Moors. Virtually independent principalities or kingdoms existed in many parts of the island, and
the rulers of these were constantly intriguing against each other.
On the whole the rulers cared little for the welfare of their
subjects. Tennent's description of them as "petty tyrants" is
justified. They were, moreover, treacherous in their dealings
with the Portuguese, cruel to their own subjects.

Reference must also be made to the devoted labours of
some of the Portuguese missionaries. The greatest tribute that
can be paid to these men is the fact that when the Portuguese
withdrew, the majority of native Roman Catholics retained
their faith though they were persecuted. The missionaries made
some small beginnings with free education. A number of schools
were established, as well as colleges and other institutions for
higher education.

The Portuguese must also be given credit for some innova-
tions in agriculture. New crops were introduced, and the

cultivation of cinnamon, areca and pepper was encouraged. Of their administrative methods nothing of value has survived. They only interfered with native customs when this was necessary for their own ends. The system of service tenure was continued. Administration of justice was crude, and trial by ordeal was permitted. Their soldiers were undisciplined, their officials corrupt. The only thing that perpetuates their name, according to one hostile Ceylonese historian, is the existence in Ceylon today of venereal disease.

CHAPTER V

THE DUTCH PERIOD, 1658-1795

I gave pepper and got ginger.—Sinhalese proverb.

BEFORE we come to consider the period of Dutch supremacy in Ceylon, it is worth examining the interesting impression of the interior of Ceylon in the second half of the seventeenth century recorded by an English sailor, Robert Knox, who was a prisoner in the island from 1660 to 1679. Knox's father was captain of a frigate which was dismasted in a cyclone off the coast of south India. The ship proceeded to Cottiar (near Trincomalee on the east coast) where Robert Knox, then nineteen years old, his father, and fourteen of the crew, were captured. It was nearly twenty years before he was to escape, but on his return to England Knox wrote a full account of conditions in Ceylon, and this was published in 1681 with the approval of the East India Company. Knox never claimed to have written "an exact and perfect treatise", but his friend Sir Christopher Wren, at that time president of the Royal Society, wrote that the book "seems to be written with great truth and integrity".

The civil government of Kandy was carried on by two chief classes of officials appointed by the king from "persons of good rank, and gentle extraction"—the Adigars, or chief judges as Knox called them, and the Dissauvas, the provincial or county governors. Subordinate to the judges and governors was the minor bureaucracy—magistrates, overseers, constables, clerks, revenue officers—who "commonly get their places by bribery".

Justice was normally administered by what Knox calls "town-consultations", that is to say, a court consisting of the local chiefs and officials. Appeals were heard by the governors, and finally by the chief justices. "But", comments Knox, "whoso gives the greatest bribe, he shall overcome." Occasionally aggrieved persons had appealed to Rajasinha, the king, but this was a risky business. Sometimes the king ordered his officials to investigate the complaint, sometimes he had the petitioners beaten and imprisoned for troubling him, and some- times he ordered the petitioners to wait until he was ready to hear their complaint, "which is not suddenly, for he is very slow in all his business. . . . They stay till they are weary, being at expense, so that the remedy is worse than the disease". Criminals could be fined, imprisoned, or forced into the army. In the event of a lawsuit, both parties to the dispute were fined. Only the king could order corporal punishment or sentence of death.

Revenue was raised in a variety of ways. On important festivals the nobility offered gifts to the king. Rents were usually paid in kind. There were certain death duties, only soldiers who died while on active service being exempt. For a time there had been a customs duty on imports from overseas, but this had been abandoned when the Dutch had occupied the main ports. The king was faced with the problem of 'incentives'—how to persuade people to work hard when their income was largely taken away in taxes. Knox describes the people as "given to sloth and laziness . . . only what their necessities force them to do, they do". But he adds: "In this I must a little vindicate them; for what indeed should they do with more than food and raiment, seeing as their estates increase, so do their taxes also?"

In one sense the law of the land was nothing more than the will of the king, but in another sense the law was composed of the vast body of recognized customs which were handed down from generation to generation and respected quite as much as if they had been codified and enforced in courts of justice. These customs dealt with a wide variety of things— inheritance, indebtedness, marriage, divorce, and so on.

The law of inheritance was complex. Normally land passed from father to sons, being divided according to the father's wishes. If, however, it was left to the eldest son, he was under an obligation to maintain his mother and any brothers or sisters who were not of age.

There was considerable indebtedness among the poorer people. A debt doubled if it were not repaid within two years, but thereafter no further interest accrued. A creditor who could not recover his debts could seize the debtor's goods. If the amount were substantial it was usual to get a licence from the local magistrate authorizing this action.

Marriages were not based on mutual affection but were arranged by the parents, "and in their choice regard more the quality and descent than the beauty". The bridegroom was expected to provide the bride's wedding dress; the bride's parents contributed as lavish a dowry of cattle, slaves or money as they could afford, and this was only returnable in the event of divorce. Divorce was by mutual consent, male children going with the man and female children with the woman. "Both women and men do commonly wed four or five times before they can settle themselves." If a woman deserted her husband, no one would marry her until her husband had re-married. Polyandry was practised on a small scale, two or more brothers sharing one wife.

The position of women was inferior to that of men. They would, for example, never sit down in the presence of a man. Yet women would talk familiarly "with any men they please, although their husbands be present". They were intensely house-proud and would put their hands to any task that needed doing.

Knox records that the children "sleep in other houses among their neighbours . . . for so they come to meet with bedfellows". Married people were equally casual in their relations with the opposite sex. It was no reproach to a married woman, he says, to have sexual relations with someone other than her husband "unless they should lay with a man of inferior quality to themselves. And the woman reckons herself as much obliged to the man for his company, as he does to her for hers. In these affairs the women are very expert. . . . If they cannot have their opportunities at home, now they appoint their meetings while the husband stays at home holding the child. . . . In some cases the men will permit their wives and daughters to lie with other men. And that is, when intimate friends or great men chance to lodge at their houses, they commonly will send their wives or daughters to bear them company in their chamber. . . . And for the matter of being with child, which many of them do not desire, they very exquisitely can prevent the same."

There was a certain amount of slavery and a man could sell himself or his children into slavery. The condition of slaves was not too severe: they could, for instance, own land or cattle. In the case of children being born as a result of a liaison between a slave and a free person, the children always took the status of the mother. The Dutch allowed slavery to continue after they had conquered the island.

There was a rigid hierarchy of ranks, a sort of caste system, based on occupation, and it was unusual for a person to marry a person of a status different from his or her own. A man might have sexual relations with a woman of lower rank but could neither eat nor drink with her. If he did so and were discovered, he would be taken before the magistrate and punished by fine or imprisonment, or both. He would, furthermore, take the same rank as the woman thereafter and would lose his family status and privileges.

The order of rank was given by Knox as follows: noblemen, goldsmiths, blacksmiths, carpenters, painters, elephant-catchers, elephant-keepers, barbers, potters, launderers, sugar-makers, farmers, soldiers, weavers, basket-makers, mat-makers, slaves, beggars. It is difficult to discover any reason for this order; why, for instance, an elephant-keeper had a higher status than a weaver, or why a farmer or soldier came lower in the scale than a launderer. It may well be that Knox went astray on the details.

Knox describes a form of 'ordeal' employed to settle questions of guilt. He writes as though this practice were unknown outside Ceylon whereas in fact it has been used at different times in almost all parts of the world and was not finally abolished by statute in Britain until the nineteenth century. The method in use in Ceylon was to plunge the hand into boiling oil: the 'ordeal' was accompanied by complicated religious ceremonial.

It is clear from Knox's account that there were many irksome restrictions imposed by the king and his officials. For instance, people who wanted to enter or leave the capital had to carry a passport, there was a complicated procedure for issuing licences for the recovery of debts, direction of labour was used for state enterprises, and there was military con scription. The collection of revenue necessitated hordes of assessment officers, customs officials, rent collectors, and tax-gatherers. There was a complicated system of justice, with different officials dealing with different types of judicial business.

The manner of life of the ordinary people was of the simplest. Their diet consisted mainly of rice, flavoured with herbs, spices or fruit juice. Meat was very scarce. The people lived in "small, low, thatched cottages, built with sticks, daubed with clay". Furniture was virtually non-existent: there would be perhaps "a stool or two without backs. . . . Tables they have none."

Yet for all the trials of living under a dictatorial and bureau-cratic government, in spite of civil war and foreign invasion, in spite of widespread ignorance, superstition, poverty, and dis-ease, Knox found the people "proper and well favoured, beyond all people that I have seen in India . . . active and nimble in their limbs: and very ingenious . . . very hardy, both for diet and weather, very proud . . . not very malicious one towards another; and their anger does not last long . . . very few spend-thrifts or bad husbands. . . ." Knox's main criticism was of the low standard of honour. "They make no account nor con-science of lying, neither is it any shame or disgrace to them, if they be catched in telling lies: it is so customary."

Most of what Knox reports is confirmed by Father Queyroz, the Portuguese priest. Queyroz describes the Sinhalese as "proud, vain and lazy"—proud because of the tradition of the celestial descent of the people, vain because of the antiquity of the nation, lazy because of the fertility of the soil. Some of their moral customs "may well be an example to us". As an illustration of this he cites their probity and horror of theft.

He says that to the Sinhalese marriage "is the greatest felicity in the world", yet there was "no stable matrimony nor union". He describes a "most barbarous custom . . . for four or five brothers or more to marry one single woman, and on the contrary one single man may marry many sisters". He confirms Knox's statement that divorce was by mutual consent, the father taking the male children and the mother the female children.

He describes the system of government as "the most tyrannical and barbarous", the king treating his subjects "worse than slaves". He explains the various forms of trial by ordeal which were used. He confirms that there was a good deal of petty litigation and that criminals with money could often buy their freedom. He gives a good deal of detailed information about the system of caste.

*   *   *   *   *

Had Rajasinha exchanged Portuguese pepper for Dutch ginger? Would he be content with the new arrangement whereby the Dutch East India Company would occupy Colombo and monopolize the island's external trade? In the event, a breach soon appeared. The day on which the Portuguese in Colombo surrendered, Rajasinha wrote a curt letter to the Dutch.

"Yesterday and the day before yesterday it was reported at our court that there was a treaty on foot with the Portuguese about the surrender of the city, since which I have received intelligence that the same is brought to effect. If it be true, you ought to have given notice thereof to our imperial majesty, which is the reason I cannot as yet give entire credit to it. But in case it should be so, I desire to know with all possible speed the articles of the said treaty. . . . I would have you remember that such as do not know God and keep their word will one time or another be sensible of the ill consequences thereof. I am sensible I have God on my side."

But the Dutch were very different from their Portuguese predecessors and thereafter behaved with great care. Their administration of Ceylon was marked by patience and industry rather than by the curious mixture of barbarism, anarchy and fanatical zeal which was characteristic of the Portuguese period.

The Dutch were soon occupied with the task of producing some sort of order out of the chaos left by the Portuguese.

Much of the country was ravaged and deserted. Demobilized native levies were given grants of land. Tamil slaves were brought from India and set to work cultivating rice. Irrigation works were restored, new crops were introduced. A sound system of administration was established, revenue was collected according to authorized regulations, and a new system of justice based on Roman-Dutch law was put into operation.

Dutch burghers (citizens) settled in large numbers and engaged in trade. Many of them married native women who had embraced the Christian religion. The Dutch governor was instructed in 1665 to see that "those who now marry native women, for want of others, educate their children well, so that in future their daughters may be married to Netherlanders, and thus our race may degenerate as little as possible". In 1678, however, the governor reported that "marriage with native women is forbidden because there is a sufficient number of women descended from European fathers". The Moors (Arabs), who had for long dominated the island's trade, were restricted to agriculture.

Rajasinha, in the meantime, was isolating himself more and more in the interior. Like all tyrants he went in constant fear of rebellion. To ensure his own safety he made frequent changes in his chief army officers and civil officials. If any nobleman seemed to become too popular or powerful, the king would have him put in prison or even executed. He made travel as difficult as possible: there was a law against felling trees in the forests, another against building bridges, and it was an offence to widen the paths and forest tracks.

The Dutch did their best to placate Rajasinha. The Dutch Governor-General of India instructed the Governor of Ceylon that "no cause of offence must be given to King Rajasinha; but rather even wrong at his hands suffered than any injury done to him". Permission was granted to send costly presents "to humour the court as much as possible". One governor remarked in an official document that very expensive presents were not really necessary but that "two or three fine Persian horses and Persian goods, some tea, porcelain, Indian preserves, etc. would be sufficient". The king was especially fond of "pictures, paintings, portraits, representations of sea battles, and snuff". Embassies bearing presents were sent to his court, and Rajasinha retained not only the presents but the ambassadors as well. Knox reports that in addition to his own English companions who had been shipwrecked at the same time, there were at the Kandyan court thirteen other English sailors, a large group of Portuguese who had chosen to live there rather than become prisoners of the Dutch, about fifty or sixty Hollanders ("Some whereof are ambassadors, some prisoners of war, some runaways, and malefactors that have escaped the hand of justice"), and eight Frenchmen. The king was glad of the presence of these Europeans, "making them his great officers". They were allowed certain privileges which were denied the other inhabitants. "He will also send for them into his presence, and discourse familiarly with them, and entertain them with great civilities."

The severity of Rajasinha's rule led to a good deal of discontent among the nobles, and in 1664 there was a revolt. It was, however, rather a Ruritanian affair. All went well at first. A small group of rebels, numbering less than 200, entered the town in which the king was residing. There was virtually no resistance. The rebels were apparently anxious to avoid harming the king, so they let him escape into the mountains. Then they proclaimed as king the youthful prince.

It was at this stage, according to Knox, that their plans went astray.

"The prince, being young and tender and having never been out of the palace, nor ever seen any but those that attended on his person, as it seemed afterwards, was scared to see so many coming and bowing down to him and telling him that he was king and his father was fled into the mountains."

There was another difficulty common in revolutionary situations. People, on the pretext that they were eliminating 'unreliable' elements, started killing their personal enemies. Old scores were paid off. Then looting began. The rebels could not agree among themselves. One of their leaders went over to Rajasinha. The situation was now out of hand, and Rajasinha had no difficulty in returning and suppressing the remnants of resistance.

The king was quite ruthless in dealing with the ringleaders. Some were executed, others imprisoned for life. He recognized that his son was a potential rival and poisoned him. Yet there is a passage in Knox's account which illustrates in a vivid way what the people of Ceylon thought about their European conquerors. After describing the king's cruelty, Knox innocently remarks that he sent one of the most noted rebels to the Dutch in Colombo, "supposing they would invent new tortures for him, beyond what he knew of". However cruel Rajasinha may have been, he recognized that when it came to "new tortures" he could not hope to rival the Europeans.

The Dutch regarded the revolt as "a gift from heaven", for its effect was to persuade Rajasinha to seek their help in restoring order. They occupied Trincomalee and Batticaloa in 1665, Kalpitiya in 1667, Cottiar in 1668. Rajasinha kept them in a state of anxiety by making informal contacts with the French and British East India Companies. The Dutch exercised great patience, even when Sinhalese troops seized their territory. Their attempts to conciliate Rajasinha continued, only to end with his death in 1687. "This exceedingly mighty king," wrote the chroniclers, "who knew how to destroy his enemies, was yet unable with all his strength and his other great qualities to gain mastery over death."

It is not certain how old Rajasinha was when he died, but he had ruled over Kandy for fifty-eight years and was probably an octogenarian. His reign had been marked by extreme despotism. His government, says Knox, was "tyrannical and arbitrary in the highest degree: for he ruleth absolutely, and after his own will and pleasure, his own head being his only counsellor".

Yet in his personal life he was curiously tolerant, even naïve. Knox says that he was indifferent to religious matters. "Of the religion of his country he makes but a small profession; as perceiving that there is a greater God than those that they, through long custom, have and do worship. . . . The Christian religion he doth not in the least persecute or dislike, but rather as it seems to me esteems and honours it." Two Roman Catholic priests had entered the king's service. Another priest, a Jesuit, had been invited by the king to do the same. "He replied to the king that he boasted more in that old habit and in the name of Jesus than in all the honour that he could do him. And so he refused the king's honour. The king valued the father for this saying." He allowed the priests to build a church, but closed it when the Portuguese "made no better than a bawdy-house of it".

He collected together a menagerie, consisting mainly of gifts of animals sent to him by the Dutch. And he treated the Europeans who fell into his hands very much as he did the animals. They were well housed and fed, and when he wanted diversion they were brought into his presence to 'perform'.

His consort came from India but, says Knox, "hath not been with him, as it is known, this twenty years. . . . He had also a daughter by her . . . that was with child by himself: but in childbed both died". Yet he was not as licentious as many monarchs of his day. "As he is abstemious in his eating, so in the use of women. If he useth them 'tis unknown and with great secrecy. . . . He allows not in his court whoredom or adultery; and many times when he hears of the misdemeanours of some of his nobles in regard of women, he not only executes them but severely punisheth the women, if known." It thus appears that he insisted on a much higher standard of sexual conduct at court than was usual in Ceylon at the time.

*   *   *   *   *

The new king was a very different person from his father. He accepted an annual subsidy from the Dutch, and left them free to conduct the entire external trade of the island. Cinnamon from the Kandyan territories was collected without difficulty. The trade in areca nuts flourished. At last Ceylon was at peace. The king wrote to the Dutch in friendly and courteous terms. The Dutch replied deferentially. The king's death in 1707 was genuinely regretted by the Dutch. He was described by a Dutchman who knew him as "very mild", displaying "much zeal for the religion, or rather the superstitions, of the country".

The new king was a boy of only seventeen years, but according to the Dutch governor had "already on various occasions shown a violent temper". His reign, which lasted more than thirty years, was also characterized by cordial relations with the Dutch. There were some disturbances especially during the second half of the reign, but on the whole a harmonious relationship was maintained. The king even went so far as to appoint the Dutch governor a member of his council.

Nevertheless, the Dutch were having their own troubles. The company's officials were engaging in private trade, to the neglect of their public duties—a difficulty which was also to trouble the British. There was a good deal of smuggling and corruption. The Dutch governor from 1702-6, Cornelis Jan Simons, devoted much care to improving the discipline and morale in the public service. He found that "many rash officials endeavoured to cover their reckless actions by the excuse of verbal orders received from my predecessor". He, therefore, made a point of issuing all important orders in writing. He found that there was "a superfluous number of clerks", that justice had been administered in a "careless manner", that several important documents were unaccountably missing from the official archives, that the schools had "fallen into decay", that the clergy had been careless in keeping accounts and had even embezzled official funds, and that in other ways administration was slack. He saw clearly the "real intentions" of his government—"what is aimed at is a monopoly in cinnamon by the exclusion of all others from its trade, both Europeans and natives". To this end he devoted himself with vigour and zeal. His successor, Hendrik Becker, also gave a good deal of attention to improving the official service. He was ruthless in dismissing incompetent or dishonest staff. When he retired he was able to report that he had worked tirelessly and had been able "to expose all the fraud and to lift the veil from the subtle mysteries presented before the eyes of rulers by dishonest servants". "Trickery and fraud" had been uprooted by "vigilance and unremitting supervision".

In 1726 a young man named Petrus Vuyst became the Dutch governor. He was a fanatical sadist, and his three years of office rivalled the worst years of Portuguese oppression. In the end he was sent home, impeached, and sentenced to death. Vuyst's period as governor did a lot of harm to the reputation of the Dutch. Floods, famine and epidemics added to the Dutch difficulties. In 1734 the trouble came to a head. The cinnamon peelers went on strike, and they were supported by the rest of the Ceylonese. The unrest spread and the Dutch had to use force, including levies from their East Indian possessions. Eventually the Dutch sent an embassy with lavish presents to the king and peace was restored. In 1739 the king died. He was the last Sinhalese king to reign in Ceylon.

The dead king's senior consort had been an Indian woman from the Malabar coast, but there was no son. The king had, therefore, nominated as his successor the brother of his senior consort. There was a good deal of discussion at the Kandyan Court because there were rival claimants to the throne. Eventually, in accordance with the king's wishes, his brother-in-law succeeded to the throne. He married a Malabar woman, and in 1751 his brother-in-law succeeded him as king, taking the title Kirti Sri. This man was not, of course, Sinhalese. His only claim to the throne of Kandy was that his Indian brother-in-law had been king before him, and his brother-in-law's only claim was that his three sisters had all been consorts of the last Sinhalese king.

It was about this time that a remarkable religious revival took place. In 1741 a deputation was sent to Burma to secure more priests who, it was hoped, would infuse new life into the decadent Buddhist hierarchy. Kirti Sri, though an alien, was determined to be a devoted servant of the religion of Kandy. He insisted that all religious festivals should be solemnly observed. He had many temples repaired, religious books copied, and himself visited some of the more sacred shrines. An embassy was sent to Siam (Thailand) and returned with more priests who were solemnly ordained in the king's presence.

Meanwhile the Dutch were having great difficulty in maintaining harmonious relations with the court at Kandy, and they submitted to repeated insults with no more than a formal protest. The king's Malabar relatives engaged in extensive smuggling. The cinnamon peelers kept going on strike. Dutch territory was seized and their forts destroyed. When messengers were sent to discuss grievances, they were severely flogged.

There were faults on both sides. Kirti Sri resented the presence of European conquerors: the Dutch governor, Jan Schreuder, behaved autocratically. A Dutch traveller has recorded the events which brought the trouble into the open. Schreuder

"formed the design of extending the cultivation of cinnamon. . . . The land on which it was supposed the cinnamon tree would thrive best was the property of the people, and possessed and inhabited by them. Without regarding the want and misery that must of necessity have overwhelmed those wretched beings if robbed of their lands, upon the produce of which they existed, the governor ordered them to give up their land and remove to a barren waste district which was appointed for them and where they might settle if they chose. These poor people, not being able to consent with indifference to leave the houses and gardens and the fields they had cultivated—all their lawful property—made many ineffectual remonstrances and sent many petitions in vain".

In desperation they appealed to Kirti Sri for his support. The king sent an ambassador to the Dutch governor, but "the haughty governor treated the ambassador with contempt, and having sent him back to his master, with an insulting answer, took possession by force of the lands of these unfortunate people". Kirti Sri, therefore, declared war on the Dutch.

Schreuder's own account of these events is very different. He found the cinnamon peelers "very untractable": the Kandyans "constantly seduced them from their duty". The king was deliberately obstructive and went out of his way to annoy the Dutch. The king was certainly autocratic. His commands, wrote an English official who met him, "are subject to no control. He has the power of life and death over his subjects, who on this account treat him with the most abject submission and approach him with a respectful kind of homage rather due to a deity than a human being".

The rebellion broke out in 1760, and for a time the Dutch were helpless. Kirti Sri openly supported the rebels. The Dutch managed to get reinforcements from India. Kirti Sri, meanwhile, had made contact with the British authorities at Madras though the negotiations were inconclusive. The Dutch campaign was badly organized but in 1765 they managed to occupy Kirti Sri's capital. The Dutch governor, records the *Culavamsa*, was "a cruel, treacherous man, low minded, and a villain. . . . The enemy hosts forced their way into the towns and destroyed the sacred books. . . . Our bold warriors, gifted with heroism, supported the king. . . . The soldiers inflicted severe losses on the enemy. . . . The hostile forces, victims of the power of infatuation, were helpless and without shelter, and came to disaster. Some were sick, some tortured by hunger and disease, some slain in battle". When the Dutch realized the impossibility of conquering Kandy, it is stated, they made amends by sending tribute to Kirti Sri, who, therefore, "pardoned their great wrong. . . . Thus was the pride of the wicked hosts of the infidel foe destroyed." Kirti Sri concluded the treaty with the Dutch in 1766. All the territory previously held by the Dutch was restored to them: in addition the entire seaboard to a depth of about four miles was ceded. The island's external trade was to be a Dutch monopoly. The Dutch agreed to defend Kandy from attack, and Kirti Sri undertook not to enter into any treaty with a foreign power. The King of Kandy was now completely isolated from foreign intercourse.

CHAPTER VI

THE BRITISH CONQUEST, 1795-1815

The scorpion stings him who helps it out of the fire.—
Tamil proverb.

THE formal British connection with Ceylon dates from the year 1762. Two years earlier revolt had broken out in Ceylon, and Kirti Sri, conscious of the weakness of his own position, sought the help of the East India Company at Madras.

The Madras Government, for its part, had every inducement to come to terms with Kandy. For one thing the British did not possess a good naval base in the Bay of Bengal. This was a serious drawback in the struggle with the French for the mastery of India, and British seamen had been casting covetous eyes at Trincomalee which was on the east coast of Ceylon. For another thing, British merchants were anxious to break the Dutch monopoly of the cinnamon trade.

So as midnight approached one rainy May night in 1762— the Kandyan monarchs always received foreign ambassadors at night—John Pybus, a member of the Madras Council, was received in audience by Kirti Sri, King of Kandy. The Kandyans wanted to know on what terms they could secure British help in their struggle with the Dutch. Pybus, who had strict instructions from the Governor of Madras not to enter into any definite commitments, merely assured the king that "the English were very desirous of cultivating his friendship and alliance". Kirti Sri and his ministers regarded this as very unsatisfactory: English friendship was no doubt desirable, but the Kandyans wanted to know what price they would have to pay for armed assistance against the Dutch. Pybus was pressed strongly on this point, and eventually put forward some tentative terms. They included the right of the East India Company to establish settlements in Ceylon, to take over the Dutch monopoly of cinnamon, pepper, and betel nut, and to control

66

the island's external trade. Kirti Sri was apparently prepared to concede all this, but the East India Company for its part was unwilling to be committed to a military alliance, and the negotiations were abandoned. A few months later the Seven Years War came to an end and Britain found herself safe in the Indian Ocean.

For almost twenty years Britain played no part in the life of Ceylon, but when towards the end of the War of American Independence the Dutch joined the coalition against Britain, the Governor of Madras decided to invade Ceylon. In January 1782 Trincomalee fell into British hands and an envoy from the Madras Government, Hugh Boyd, thought by some to be author of the *Letters of Junius*, was sent to Kandy. Boyd arrived at an unfortunate moment. King Kirti Sri had just died from injuries caused by a fall from his horse and had been succeeded by his brother. Boyd proposed an alliance against the Dutch, but the new king, remembering how his brother's overtures had been unsuccessful twenty years before, expressed the friendliest sentiments but refused to negotiate a treaty. Boyd was given a letter to take back to the Governor of Madras. "It contained", recorded Boyd in his journal, "the strongest assurances of the friendly disposition of His Majesty towards the English. . . . It expressed his anxious desire to establish a connection and alliance, as proposed by the Government of Madras. But that to make the alliance sufficiently firm and respectable for him to accede to, it would be necessary to procure to it the sanction of the King of England, signified *under his own hand.*" Boyd had to return empty-handed.

As it happened Trincomalee was not long in British hands. It was captured by the French in August 1782, and restored to the Dutch.

For a dozen years Britain paid no attention to Ceylon, but in 1793 France declared war against Britain and the following year invaded Holland where they set up a government friendly to themselves. The Dutch in Ceylon were in an acutely difficult position. The Prince of Orange, a refugee in England, instructed the Dutch Governor of Ceylon to co-operate with the British. At first it seemed as if the wishes of the Prince of Orange would be respected, but later information from Holland which reached the Dutch in Ceylon suggested that the change of government at home carried fairly general support. Eventually the Dutch decided to resist any British encroachments. The British, therefore, proceeded to the use of force. Trincomalee was captured in August 1795, and Jaffna in September. The following February Colombo was surrendered, due partly to the weakening of the garrison which occurred when a regiment of Swiss mercenaries under a certain Comte de Meuron transferred its allegiance to Britain.

Meanwhile negotiations had again been opened with the King of Kandy. The British envoy, Robert Andrews of the Madras Service, had made two main proposals—a joint British-Kandyan attack on Colombo, and a British monopoly of the cinnamon trade. The King of Kandy accepted the conditions and a draft treaty was concluded. The treaty was, however, never ratified by the Kandyans and accordingly lapsed.

The question of the future of Ceylon immediately arose. Was it to be restored to the Dutch when the war ended or should it become a British colony? There were advocates of both courses. As a temporary expedient the island was administered by the Madras Government.

The people of Ceylon had no doubt been glad to see the end of Dutch rule, but that did not make them welcome the advent of the British. The fact was that Britain acquired Ceylon more to deny its use to the French than for any positive purpose. It was part of what Sir John Seely described as "a fit of absence of mind". Like Burma in later years, Ceylon was administered as if it were a dependency of India for no better reason than that it had been conquered by troops from India.

The British were soon immersed in administrative difficulties. The defeated Dutch had no reason to make the task of the British easy. Some of the Ceylonese, it is true, were willing to co-operate with the new administration, but they were often criticized by their fellow-countrymen for being guilty of what our generation calls 'collaborationist activities'.

Furthermore nobody knew how long the British intended to stay in Ceylon, and until the decision not to restore the island to the Dutch was taken, many important questions had to be left undecided.

But the greatest difficulty was the fact that the officials sent to administer the island were, for the most part, ignorant of the languages and customs. In our day intense preparations are made during time of war so that liberated or occupied territory shall be administered by experienced persons possessing some knowledge of conditions obtaining in the territory. Such a conception would have seemed absurd to the British soldier at the end of the eighteenth century. War was limited, in his mind, to the task of conquest or subjugation, and it was typical of the times that the Colonial Office was an offshoot of the War Department, and remained so until as late as 1854. Even if the British had realized that a thorough understanding of local languages and conditions was essential to efficient administration, the fact was that there were virtually no British officials or soldiers who possessed the necessary knowledge. An attempt might have been made to utilize some at least of the minor Dutch and Ceylonese officials who had been employed under the Dutch governors. Such a course no doubt had its dangers, but it might have been tried. Instead, British and Indian officials were imported from Madras. Even then the situation might have been saved if they had made an effort to understand local conditions and customs. This they failed to do. It was decided that the easier policy was to enforce the system of administration which had been used in Madras. Native customs and prejudices were ignored, and when a tax on coco-nut trees was introduced, opposition to British policy came to a head. Soon the island was in revolt. Some of the Dutch in the island took advantage of the situation to create more disorder, and some of the Ceylonese who had held official posts under the Dutch also encouraged the revolt. The trouble began about the middle of 1797 and lasted until February or March the following year. The advantage was with the rebels who knew the country and could rely on the backing of the local population.

The obviously unsatisfactory nature of the Madras Government's administration was causing serious misgivings in London. Critics of William Pitt seized on every bit of evidence of inefficiency or misfortune in order to embarrass the government. There was, however, no question of returning the island to the Dutch. The East India Company was resolutely opposed to any such course, and in any case the attitude of the Dutch in Ceylon to the disturbances of 1797-8 had created a bad impression in Britain.

At first it was suggested that the island should become a crown colony, but the East India Company regarded this as almost as unwelcome as returning Ceylon to the Dutch. Finally, a compromise was agreed upon: the island was to be administered jointly by the East India Company and the Imperial Government. It was a compromise doomed to failure from the start. Joint administration meant joint responsibility. Who was responsible for the policies adopted? Who was to be blamed if mistakes were made? An attempt was made to define the functions of the two authorities. General administration was to be in the hands of officials appointed from Britain, while the collection of revenue and the control of commerce was to be left to the East India Company.

The period of dual control began in October 1798, when the Hon. Frederick North arrived in Ceylon and assumed office as governor. From the start it was impossible to determine where responsibility for the island's administration really lay. Ultimate authority was no doubt with the President of the Board of Control for the Affairs of India (at that time Henry Dundas, later to become the first Viscount Melville). North, as governor, was, however, under the immediate control of the Governor-General of India, Marquess Wellesley, and the directors of the East India Company. Wellesley and the directors were themselves at loggerheads. Wellesley maintained a regular correspondence with his friends in the Ministry at home, to one of whom he described the directors as a "pack of narrow-minded old women". He was attacked in Parliament, one Member alleging that "though he was solemnly sworn to obey the instructions of his employers . . . yet instead of so doing, on his arrival in India, he disregarded their authority, disobeyed their instructions, assumed to himself a despotic power, turned his back upon the true interests of the company, and did without their permission and contrary to their instructions, for the gratification of his own caprice, with the most flagitious profusion, and for corrupt purposes, squander the money of the said company to an enormous extent". His brother, Sir Arthur Wellesley (later to become Duke of Wellington), entered the British Parliament in 1806 specifically in order to defend his brother's reputation.

North himself did not possess the right sort of temperament for the exceedingly difficult job which faced him. He was a versatile man with a great deal of personal charm, and he had the best intentions in the world: but he was impetuous and often unwise in his actions. He began by appointing those Sinhalese of good character who had held office under the Dutch to fill the places of the Indians who had returned to Madras. This, in itself, was a wise move as none of the British officials spoke the native languages, and the co-operation of educated Ceylonese was essential if the administration was to be successful.

From the start North had to contend with the unconcealed hostility of the Madras officials, who resented the fact that administration was not the exclusive responsibility of the Madras Government. He soon came to the conclusion that he would have to suspend Robert Andrews who had been in charge of the civil administration during the period of Madras rule. This was no doubt inevitable, for Andrews was not the man to accept his new subordinate position gracefully. The result, however, was to increase the hostility of the Madras clique towards North.

At first North relied a good deal on Hugh Cleghorn, the Colonial Secretary. Cleghorn was an odd character. He had at one time been a professor at St. Andrew's University and had later served in the British Secret Service. In 1799 North was told that Cleghorn was implicated in a conspicuous piece of corruption in connection with the pearl fisheries. North had the matter investigated and it was clear that even if Cleghorn were guiltless of dishonest conduct, he had been extremely negligent in not preventing corruption in his subordinates. He was suspended in December 1799.

This was not all, however. John Macdowall, Collector of Colombo, was dismissed for his failure to co-operate with North; I. Garrow, Collector of Batticaloa, was suspended for "arbitrary injustice"; Edward Atkinson, Paymaster General of the troops, kept false accounts and was allowed to resign; Gavin Hamilton, Atkinson's successor, was found, after his

death, to have embezzled some £20,000 of public money; and
George Melville Leslie, Hamilton's successor, was also guilty
of malversation and was relieved of his post. Such conduct,
besides being acutely embarrassing to North, created a most
unfortunate impression on the people of Ceylon.

North's propensity to take hasty and ill-considered action
is illustrated by his policy in connection with land tenure. In
1796 the traditional 'Service Tenure' system had been abandoned in favour of a tax of 50 per cent of the value of the
produce of the land. A Committee of Investigation, presided
over by de Meuron, the commander of the Swiss regiment
which transferred its allegiance to Britain in 1797, had considered the matter in 1797 and had recommended a return to
'Service Tenure'. "The more our system approximates to that
heretofore in force (always supposing the abuses of its administration corrected) the better it will apply to this island where,
from the . . . long established prejudices of the natives, many
of those customs and laws which to a stranger may appear
impolitic and oppressive are in reality gratifying to the people,
and necessary to the welfare and security of the State." Accordingly the 'Service Tenure' system was again adopted. North,
however, took an instinctive dislike to the system. It was, he
thought, offensive to "men of liberal sentiments and en-
lightened minds". He persuaded himself that the people would
welcome the abolition of a custom which he himself considered
degrading. Ignoring all the advice he received from his colleagues, North, by proclamation in 1800, abolished 'Service
Tenure'.

North's civil administration was not, however, a complete
failure. The code of law was revised, and new courts were
established. A revised revenue system was adopted. Education
was revived, and by 1801 there were 170 schools—in spite of
the fact that North had been instructed by the Government in London not to spend more than £1,500 a year on
education.

It was, however, inevitable that dual control would have
to be abandoned. Dundas came to this view in the second year
of North's administration, and on 1st January, 1802, the share
of the East India Company in the administration of Ceylon

came to an end and the island became a Crown Colony. At the same time, by the Treaty of Amiens, the Dutch ceded and guaranteed "in full property and sovereignty, to his Brittanic Majesty, all the possessions and establishments in the island of Ceylon, which previous to the war belonged to the Republic of the United Provinces, or to the Dutch East India Company".

There were two immediate advantages from the change in administration. In the first place, responsibility for administration was now clearly laid down. Details were settled by the governor and him alone, and general questions of policy were decided by Lord Hobart (later Earl of Buckinghamshire), the Secretary of State for the Colonial and War Departments in London. Secondly, it was now possible to create a separate Ceylon civil service. Until then the majority of posts had been filled from the Madras Service, an arrangement which North found extremely irksome. Ceylon was very much of a 'poor relation', and few Madras officials of ability would willingly accept a transfer to Ceylon. In order to compensate the civil servants for the low rate of salaries, North allowed them to supplement their official incomes by engaging in trade and cultivating land. He also created new posts, frequently sinecures, so that his most valuable officials could increase their incomes by holding several posts simultaneously. The governor remained the sole repository of executive, legislative, and judicial authority, but an advisory council, consisting of a number of senior officials, was created. The governor was expected to consult this council on important matters, though he was not bound by the advice he received.

The first years of crown colony status were disturbed by a series of disastrous encounters with the Kandyan kingdom. Britain, it will be remembered, was in occupation of the maritime provinces and Kandy remained—as it had during the Portuguese and Dutch occupations—nominally independent. The draft treaty of 1795 had never been ratified on the Kandyan side and had accordingly lapsed. In 1798 the king died without legitimate issue. The First Adigar, or Chief Minister, whose name was Pilama Talauve, was the most powerful person in the kingdom, "a man of equal ambition and artifice", according to a contemporary. This Adigar was a Kandyan nobleman who had toyed with the idea of ending the alien Malabar dynasty by seizing power himself. The opposition of the Kandyan nobility led him to postpone this plan. Instead he placed on the throne a young and weak prince whom he hoped to dominate and eventually overthrow. This prince took the title Sri Vikrama Rajasinha. The rest of the royal family were thrown into prison by the Adigar, though the former king's brother-in-law, Muttusami, managed to escape and sought refuge in British territory.

The Adigar now decided to seek British support in his plan to seize the throne. He arranged a meeting with North and complained of the new king's conduct. He suggested that the British should depose the king and that he himself should be placed on the throne. North indignantly rejected the suggestion. Pilama Talauve's next proposal was that he should persuade the king to attack the British, who would thereupon occupy Kandy and place him on the throne. North's reply was that he would hold Pilama Talauve responsible if war broke out. The Adigar then put forward a third plan. The king's formal title to rule should be untouched but the effective government should be in his own hands. He would request British protection, and the result would be that British control of the whole of the island would be secure.

North was in some difficulty. He took the view that the existence of a semi-independent kingdom in the interior was a threat to the British position in the maritime provinces. He was, moreover, inclined to believe the Adigar's reports about the unpopularity of the Malabar king and was attracted by the idea of giving effective power to the Adigar who was, after all, a Kandyan. On the other hand he suspected that the Adigar was a rogue, and he was determined that no change in the government of Kandy should be made without the king's consent. For a time he vacillated. One day he would be so filled with horror at the Adigar's duplicity that he would be certain that no co-operation was possible. The next day he would be equally sure that without the Adigar's co-operation Britain could never be secure in Ceylon. Such was his lack of confidence in his own judgment that he wrote to Wellesley: "I am not sure whether I have acted like a good politician or like a great nincompoop". Impulsive and a bad judge of character, North eventually decided on co-operation with the Adigar. He told the Adigar that if the king would agree, Kandy should become a British protectorate. The king would remain titular head of the kingdom, but the real ruler would be Pilama Talauve. A draft treaty was drawn up and an ambassador, General Macdowall, with an escort of 1,200 troops, set out for Kandy with the Adigar as guide. North told the ambassador privately that if the king would not accept the proposed arrangement, it was to be assumed that the king and not the Adigar was the real ruler and the plan should, therefore, be abandoned. This, in fact, happened. The king refused to agree to North's proposals, and the British Ambassador withdrew without forcing the issue.

It was not until 1802 that the Adigar achieved his objective. In April a group of his hirelings seized a consignment of areca nuts belonging to some merchants from Puttalam. North endeavoured to secure compensation, but without success. Early in 1803 British troops invaded the Kandyan kingdom.

The British commander set off from Colombo with nearly 2,000 men, and a second column of about 1,400 men left Trincomalee a few days later. By the end of three weeks the two columns had arrived in Kandy, finding it deserted and in flames. North decided to place on the throne Muttusami, the brother-in-law of the previous king—a man of doubtful character—who had escaped from prison and had been living at Jaffna under British protection for several years. It was hoped, to quote the Rev. James Cordiner, chaplain to the Colombo garrison at the time, "that, through his influence, the army would be supplied with provisions, and matters arranged in the territories without bloodshed, agreeably to the wishes of our government". Muttusami, who had for some time laid claim to the throne of Kandy, agreed to North's plan.

Pilama Talauve, who had fled with the king and the court to the jungle, now made secret contact with the British. He suggested that the new British-sponsored king, Muttusami, should be deposed, and that real power should be placed in his own hands. It was at this point that North made his greatest blunder. He concluded a convention with the Adigar which provided that Muttusami, who only a few weeks earlier had been placed on the throne, should deliver over the administration of Kandy to Pilama Talauve who would be invested with the title of Grand Prince. Muttusami would "reside and hold his court at Jaffnapatam". The rightful king, who had taken refuge in the jungle, was to be delivered into British hands. This convention being concluded, the British general departed for Colombo leaving in Kandy a garrison of 300 Europeans, 700 Malay levies, a few Indian troops, and some sick and wounded.

North now decided to embark on a tour of inspection of the new protectorate, in the course of which he met Pilama Talauve and personally confirmed the terms of the truce. The Adigar had toyed with the idea of kidnapping North during this interview, but at the last minute he abandoned this plan. The British general returned to Kandy to arrange the details of the truce. He was soon taken ill with fever and returned to Colombo.

The Adigar's troops now surrounded the British garrison at Kandy. After some days of fighting the British were forced to capitulate. Under the terms of the surrender it was agreed that the British should hand over Kandyan territory to Pilama Talauve and that the new king, Muttusami, should leave Kandy. On 24th June, 1803, the British party left, but only one member of the party, a corporal called George Barnsley, escaped to recount the story of the massacre. He describes how the Kandyans took the soldiers two by two, "knocked them down with the butt-end of their pieces, and beat out their brains". Barnsley himself received the same treatment as the others but was not actually killed. He "lay as dead for some time" and was stripped of his clothing. When it was dark he crawled into the bushes, supporting his half-severed head with his hands. Painfully and slowly he made his way back to British territory.

The massacre at Kandy led the British to adopt retaliatory tactics. "You will, in conjunction with other detachments," wrote the British commander to one of his officers, "concert such measures as will best tend to effect the greatest devastation and injury to the enemy's country".

The Kandyan War of 1803 was, of course, the subject of

much controversy in the United Kingdom. Thomas Creevey, M.P. for Thetford, had raised the matter in Parliament in March 1804. The war, he said, had arisen merely because of the seizure by some Kandyan officials of a consignment of areca nuts belonging to a British merchant. "Our government claimed the property, and it was agreed to be restored or the value to be paid. . . . The first difference between the English and Kandyan Governments was whether this sum of £300 should be paid instantly or at the expiration of a few months. . . . It was in this transaction that our national honour was supposed to be involved." Viscount Castlereagh, President of the Board of Control for the Affairs of India, claimed in reply that "the value is of little consequence; the Kandyan Government has long demonstrated an hostile mind towards us".

Creevey described the war as "rank and impolitic in its origin and commencement . . . calamitous in its consequences", and laid the main blame at the door of North: but he also complained that Henry Addington's Government had not informed Parliament of the facts. Castlereagh replied in the familiar phrase that it was not in the public interest to disclose the information. Charles James Fox immediately rose. "It is really extraordinary," he said, "to hear Ministers resisting the production of information on a subject where the necessity of information is admitted by every description of mankind who choose for a moment to exercise their judgment. If this is not the moment for inquiry, I wish to know when that moment will arrive? Does the noble lord mean to say that no inquiry will be made till the conclusion of the war? If that is to be the case, the grand object of the motion will be lost. Nothing can then be gained but the punishment of the criminal party." Addington urged that judgment should be deferred until more information was available, and Creevey's motion was lost.

The Opposition in England had maintained that the war was unnecessary but that British honour could only be secured by a punitive expedition. This, however, was quite out of the question and in fact it was the Kandyans who were attacking. Their forces invaded British territory and actually penetrated to within a few miles of Colombo. Gradually, as small numbers of British reinforcements reached Ceylon, the Kandyans were

ejected. Border warfare continued desultorily. It was conducted,
wrote a British officer, "by both parties, Christian and Heathen,
with savage barbarity".

In July 1805 North was succeeded as governor by Sir
Thomas Maitland. The change of governor was not caused
primarily because of any dissatisfaction at home with the conduct of the Kandyan war but because of an unseemly personal
dispute between North and his commander-in-chief. Although
it was clear that North alone was responsible for the general
conduct of policy in Ceylon, there was no clear allocation of
responsibility for the detailed administration of civil and
military matters, a common cause of trouble in the early stages
of the occupation of a country after war. No difficulties had
arisen on this score during the greater part of North's period
of governorship, though this was more due to the friendly
personal relations between North and General Macdowall than
to any precision in defining the two spheres of authority. In
1804, however, Macdowall had been succeeded by General
Wemyss, a stubborn, domineering and overweening individual.
The war with Kandy was in progress at the time, and Wemyss
regarded this as his own private venture. He refused to discuss
his plans with North, and incurred expenditure far beyond
what the civil government had provided for. North was in a
very delicate position; every complaint of extravagance was met
by Wemyss with the plea of military necessity. Soon the whole
official community was taking sides in the dispute, and energy
which might have been used in prosecuting the Kandyan War
was wasted in fruitless antagonism and petty jealousy. The
climax came over a ridiculous dispute about a small piece of
land at Colombo which was claimed by both the army and the
Supreme Court. North intervened and ordered Wemyss to
vacate the land. Wemyss ostentatiously withdrew, announcing
that the safety of Colombo was now in North's hands since he
no longer had any authority there. No sooner was this incident
over than Wemyss was brought before the Supreme Court on
a charge of contempt. The dispute had now become so absurd
that no solution was possible without a complete change of
personnel, and North and Wemyss were both recalled.

A change of governor was certainly overdue, and it was

drastic enough when it came. Nobody could have been more
unlike his predecessor than was Sir Thomas Maitland. He was
a professional soldier of wide experience, having served in
Europe and Asia. He had for a time been Member of Parliament for Haddington. He was undoubtedly an able person,
but he was autocratic, somewhat quarrelsome, and certainly
eccentric, and was known by his subordinates as 'King Tom'.
Sir Charles Napier described him as "a rough old despot . . .
with talent, but not of a first-rate order, narrow-minded, seeing
many things under false lights . . . surrounded by sycophants,
who thought him a god because he had more intelligence than
they". He was in Ceylon for only five years, but during that
time the administration of the island was transformed.

For six months Maitland initiated no drastic changes. He
studied the island's problems diligently, consulting those who
knew local conditions. He then devoted his attention to the
civil service. He took the view that general progress was
impossible until there existed a civil service that was efficient,
incorruptible, and hard working. He was ruthless in his attempt
to achieve this. He put a stop to the practice—which North
had permitted—of officials engaging in trade, and he abolished
all posts he considered unnecessary. At the same time he
increased the salaries so that no official was driven to supplement his income by illicit activities. Officials who learnt a
native language received quicker promotion than those who
only knew English. He put a stop to corruption and nepotism.
He inaugurated a system of strict control over public expenditure and appointed a Commissioner of Revenue with duties
in some ways analogous to those now performed by the
Comptroller and Auditor General in the United Kingdom.
'Service Tenure' was restored and native headmen were given
certain responsibilities for maintaining order. The judicial
system was improved, and trial by jury introduced. Disabilities
on Roman Catholics were removed. The East India Company
regulation which prevented Europeans from occupying land
outside Colombo was abandoned, with the result that many
new cinnamon plantations were started.

Maitland quickly came to three conclusions about Kandy.
First, that without large-scale British reinforcements—which

were not forthcoming—it would be impossible to subjugate
Kandy. Second, that subjugation was unnecessary because the
existence of a semi-independent kingdom in the jungles of
central Ceylon in no way threatened Britain's position in the
maritime provinces. Third, that the Adigar was an unscrupulous
rascal with whom no agreement was possible. Kandy, he wrote,

"is infinitely beneath contempt. . . . It is not the Kandyans
that are formidable, but Mr. North's opinions on the subject
that have rendered them formidable. The great fault was,
from the commencement, regarding them as a regular power.
Had I so considered them, I might have gone to war with
them every day since I came here. . . . The king would always
quarrel with whatever power held the coast; so that unless
we mean to extinguish him (which we certainly were not
strong enough to attempt), our only possible course was to
ignore the affronts that he offered us, and to find our con-
solation in keeping the peace, even if it were rather an
ignoble one."

Maitland put these conclusions to the test and fighting ceased,
though without a formal treaty.

The King of Kandy, Sri Vikrama Rajasinha, realized the
insecurity of his own position. His Chief Adigar had shown
himself to be self-seeking and disloyal. For some years they
both manœuvred for position, but in 1811 Pilama Talauve
was suspected of being involved in a plot to assassinate the
king, found guilty, and beheaded. He was succeeded as Chief
Adigar by his nephew Ehelapola. This man, too, conspired
against the king, was discovered, and fled to Colombo. The
story is that his children were publicly beheaded in front of
the palace at Kandy and that his wife, under threat of being
publicly raped, was compelled to pound the severed heads of
her children with a pestle and was then drowned in a nearby
lake.

Sri Vikrama Rajasinha, who had succeeded to the throne
as an inexperienced youth some fifteen years earlier, had from
the start faced the hostility of his own officials and the Kandyan
nobility. He had gone in constant fear of his life, and fear had

bred cruelty. A British officer who met him several times describes him as "dignified" and "affable". "Having been placed on the throne by a professed friend, but in reality an inveterate intriguing enemy, for the intriguer's own aggrandizement, his situation as king was attended with insuperable difficulties. . . . He lived under the constant fear of conspiracies. . . . He never retired to rest without the fear of assassination. Fear produces oppression, and oppression excites fear." As his reign progressed he became more and more despotic. "He destroyed his subjects like a devil," it is stated in the *Culavamsa*. "He had many hundreds of people impaled in a merciless death. Like a thief that robs villages, he confiscated much wealth that had come to the people by inheritance. And because he committed many evil deeds, the Sinhalese and the inhabitants of Colombo [the British] rebelled. They came hither and captured the criminal king alive." The vicious treatment he is supposed to have meted to Ehelapola's relatives was the act which brought about his own downfall, though it was in fact several months before the British intervened. Then, in 1814, to quote Sir Emerson Tennent, "a party of native merchants, British subjects, who had gone up to Kandy to trade, were seized and mutilated by the tyrant; they were deprived of their ears, their noses, and hands, and those who survived were driven towards Colombo, with the severed members tied to their necks".

The governor, Sir Robert Brownrigg, who had succeeded Maitland, decided that the time had come to put an end to the reign of terror. He issued a proclamation in January 1815 stating that he:

"could not hear with indifference the prayers of the inhabitants of five extensive provinces, constituting more than one-half of the Kandyan kingdom, who with one unanimous voice raised against the tyranny and oppression of their ruler . . . implored the protection of the British Government. . . . Neither could His Excellency contemplate without the liveliest emotions of indignation and resentment, the atrocious barbarity recently perpetrated in Kandy upon ten innocent subjects of the British Government, seven of whom died instantly of their sufferings, and three miserable

F

victims were sent, in defiance, with their mutilated limbs across the limits, to relate the distressing tale, and exhibit the horrid spectacle to the eyes of an insulted government, and an indignant people. . . . His Excellency has become convinced of the unavoidable necessity of resolving to carry His Majesty's arms into the Kandyan country. . . . But it is not against the Kandyan nation that the arms of His Majesty are directed. His Excellency proclaims hostility against that tyrannical power alone which has provoked by aggravated outrages and indignities the just resentment of the British nation. . . . His Excellency hereby proffers to every individual of the Kandyan nation the benign protection of the British Government."

This time the invasion was carefully planned, but it was not an invasion so much as a triumphal march. The British troops were acclaimed by the officials and nobles as liberators rather than conquerors. Not one British soldier was killed in action. Within a few weeks Kandy was occupied and the king captured and sent into exile in India. The British conquest of Ceylon was complete.

CHAPTER VII

FROM THE KANDYAN WAR TO THE
COLEBROOKE COMMISSION, 1815-1832

*The bat that has come to the house of another must
remain suspended.*—Sinhalese proverb.

THE Kandyan War came to a formal end by the Convention
of 2nd March, 1815. The relation of Kandy to the rest of
Ceylon has created so many problems, some of them still unsolved, that it is worth examining the terms of the convention
with care. The following extracts contain the main points.

"... *it is agreed and established as follows:*
1st. That the cruelties and oppressions of the Malabar
Ruler in the arbitrary and unjust affliction of bodily tortures
and the pains of Death without Trial and sometimes without
an accusation or the possibility of a crime, and in the general
contempt and contravention of all Civil Rights have become
flagrant, enormous and intolerable, the acts and maxims of
His Government being equally and entirely devoid of that
Justice which should secure the safety of his subjects, and
of that good faith which might obtain a beneficial intercourse
with the neighbouring settlements.
2nd. That the Rajah Sri Wikreme Rajah Sinha by the
habitual violation of the chief and most sacred duties of a
Sovereign, has forfeited all claims to that title or the powers
annexed to the same, and is declared fallen and deposed
from the Office of King—His family and relatives ... for
ever excluded from the throne—and all claim and title of
the Malabar race to the dominion of the Kandyan Provinces
is abolished and extinguished.
3rd. That all male persons being or pretending to be
relations of the late Rajah ... are hereby declared enemies
to the Government of the Kandyan Provinces and excluded

83

and prohibited from entering those Provinces on any pretext whatever, without a written permission for that purpose by the authority of the British Government. . . .

4th. The Dominion of the Kandyan Provinces is vested in the Sovereign of the British Empire. . . . Saving to the Adigars . . . and all other chief and subordinate Native Headmen, lawfully appointed by authority of the British Government, the Rights, Privileges and Powers of their respective Offices, and to all classes of the people the Safety of their persons and property, with their Civil rights and immunities, according to the laws, institutions and customs established and in force amongst them.

5th. The Religion of Boodhoo [Buddha] . . . is declared inviolable, and its Rites, Ministers and Places of worship are to be maintained and protected.

6th. Every species of bodily torture, and all mutilation of limb, member or organ, are prohibited and abolished.

7th. No sentence of Death can be carried into execution against any inhabitant except by the written Warrant of the British Governor or Lieut.-Governor for the time being. . . .

8th. Subject to these Conditions, the administration of Civil and Criminal Justice and Police over the Kandyan inhabitants of the said Provinces is to be exercised according to established Forms and by the ordinary authorities, saving always the inherent Right of Government to redress grievances and reform abuses. . . .

11th. The Royal Dues and Revenues of the Kandyan Provinces are to be managed and collected for His Majesty's use and the support of the Provincial Establishment. . . ."

The Kandyan problem of today derives from the fact that "the Kandyan kingdom finally became subject to the British Commonwealth, not by right of conquest as did the remainder of Ceylon, but as a result of a treaty by which its integrity, liberty, institutions, laws and religion were to be guaranteed by the British Government". (Report of the Soulbury Commission, 1945.) We shall be returning to this matter later and it will be useful to bear in mind the circumstances under which Kandy was annexed, and the terms of the convention.

Sir Robert Brownrigg, who became governor in 1811, decided to keep the administration of Kandy quite distinct from that of the rest of Ceylon. A resident was appointed and made a member of the governor's advisory council. A board of commissioners to assist the resident was appointed in 1816. Local administration was left to Kandyan nobles, who were made provincial governors. For a time all seemed well. Indeed, Brownrigg wrote to the Secretary of State: "A musical clock . . . was presented by Mr. D'Oyly to the temple . . . and gave infinite satisfaction, both as a mark of favour from the British Government and for its curiosity. The chimes excited surprise and admiration." But the atmosphere of peace and co-operation was superficial and a comparatively minor incident in 1817 led to a rebellion which was at one time so serious that a British evacuation of the island was seriously contemplated.

The main underlying causes of the revolt were twofold. First, the Kandyan nobles were given too much power, and were not adequately supervised by the few British officials. Second, the British underestimated the power of the hierarchy of the Buddhist religion. The priests were constantly intriguing to expel the British. The Kandyans, commented one British observer, "showed no dislike to us individually, but as a nation they abhorred us. . . . They made no complaint of oppression or misrule, contenting themselves with expressing a wish that we should leave the country".

The spark which ignited the gunpowder hardly seemed important at the time. A former priest named Wilbawe claimed the Kandyan throne and, with a few other priests and personal friends, established himself in the jungle. His activities were not at first taken seriously, but when Wilbawe began inciting the people to revolt, the assistant resident at Badulla decided to act and in October 1817 sent a couple of dozen Malay soldiers to arrest the pretender. Wilbawe and his friends resisted and the assistant resident was killed.

This was the signal for revolt which, within six months, had spread throughout almost the whole of Kandy. With the single exception of a man called Molligoda, who had been Chief Adigar under the last Kandyan king, every noble of note either joined the rebels or was arrested by the British. Fuel was added to the flames in May 1818 when a priest removed the Sacred Tooth of the Buddha from Kandy and took it to the rebel leaders. The significance of this incident was the Kandyan belief that whoever held the Sacred Tooth was the rightful ruler.

The Kandyans had considerable advantages. They knew the terrain and were able to adopt guerrilla tactics. They avoided open combat, merely harassing the British forces from jungle hide-outs. That the British were able to suppress the revolt was due as much as anything to Kandyan dissensions. One of the leaders of the revolt who at first thought that Wilbawe had a title to the throne came to the conclusion in September 1818 that Wilbawe was after all an impostor. He therefore seized him and replaced him with a pretender of his own choice. By the end of October the revolt had collapsed and the ring-leaders were court martialled and beheaded. The rebellion was suppressed only "after severe British losses had been incurred and the Kandyans had been treated with a severity difficult to justify". (Report of the Donoughmore Commission, 1928.) "The houses of the inhabitants were forthwith set on fire and burnt to the ground," wrote a British officer, "and all the cattle, grain, etc., belonging to the people destroyed. The inhabitants appeared to be horror-struck at the devastation. . . . Much care was taken to sweep the country bare of everything, for the purpose of depriving the inhabitants of the means of sub-sistence. . . . White and black races, the invaded and the in-vaders, Christian and pagan, vied with each other in promoting the horrors and barbarities of mutual destruction."

When it was certain that the rebellion was over, Brownrigg issued a Proclamation. This Proclamation (November 1818) recorded the circumstances of the Rajah's deposition and the cession of Kandy. It then recounted the benefits of the British administration.

"The exercise of Power by the Representative of His Britannic Majesty . . . was marked with the greatest mild-ness and forbearance towards all Classes; the strictest atten-tion to the protection and maintenance of the Rights, Minis-ters and Places of Worship of the Religion of Boodhoo; and a general deference to the Opinions of the Chiefs. . . . In exacting either Taxes or Services for the state an extraordinary and unprecedented laxity was allowed. . . .

Under this mild Administration on the part of the British Government the Country appeared to rest in Peace . . . yet all this time there were factions and intriguing spirits at work seeking for an opportunity to subvert the Government. . . . These Plotters against the State were found among the very Persons who had been restored to Honours and Security by the sole intervention of British Power. . . . After more than a year of conflict which has created misery and brought destruction on many, the efforts of the British Government and the bravery of His Majesty's Troops have made manifest in the Kandyans the folly of resistance. . . .

His Excellency the Governor therefore now calls to the mind of every person and of every Class within these Settlements, that the Sovereign Majesty of the King of Great Britain and Ireland exercised by His Representative the Governor of Ceylon and his Agents in the Kandyan Provinces is the source alone from which all Power emanates, and to which obedience is due: that no Chief who is not vested with Authority or Rank from this Sovereign source is entitled to obedience or Respect; and that without Powers derived from Government, no one can exercise Jurisdiction of any kind or inflict the slightest Punishment. And finally that every Kandyan be he of the highest or lowest Class, is secured in his Life, Liberty and Property from encroachment of any kind or by any Person, and is only subject to the Laws which will be administered according to the Ancient and established usages of the Country, and in such manner and by such Authorities and Persons as in the Name and on behalf of His Majesty is herein declared."

The Proclamation then outlined in detail the form of government which was to be established, and the duties and privileges of various classes of persons. It prescribed the authority of the Board of Commissioners; the appointment and duties of ministers, provincial governors and headmen; the honours to be paid to different classes of people ("But all

Chiefs and other persons coming before, meeting or passing
any British Officer, Civil or Military, of Rank and Authority
in the Island of Ceylon, shall give up the middle of the Road,
and if sitting rise and make a suitable Obeisance"); the protection not only of the Buddhist but of all religions; the assessment
of taxes and collection of revenue; the prohibition of gifts to
officials; the maintenance of roads and bridges, and the performance of other services; the administration of justice and
the maximum penalties which could be inflicted. The conclud-
ing article reads: "In all matters not provided for by this
Proclamation or other Proclamations heretofore promulgated
by the Authority of the British Government, His Excellency
reserves to himself and his successors the Power of reforming
Abuses and making such Provision as is necessary, beneficial
or desirable. He also reserves full power to alter the present
Provision as may appear hereafter necessary and expedient. . . ."

The Proclamation of 1818 is a very different document
from the Convention of 1815. It is a unilateral declaration of
British policy whereas the Convention was a treaty adhered to
by the Adigars and provincial governors as well as by the
British governor. Its tone is imperious and peremptory, whereas
the Convention was friendly and sympathetic. It outlines in
considerable detail the form of government to be established,
whereas the Convention merely records general principles and
the determination to maintain traditional institutions. Furthermore the Proclamation specifically reserves the right of the
British Government to amend the Proclamation in whatever
way might seem necessary and expedient.

The British view at the time was that the Convention of
1815 had become a dead letter by the action of the Kandyan
signatories during the rebellion of 1817–18. The Kandyan
chiefs have always denied this contention. They

"claim that the Proclamation issued by the Governor after
the rebellion in 1818 confirmed the spirit, if it modified the
letter, of the Convention. They have, moreover, no difficulty
in producing evidence to show that the Government, in
spite of its subsequent actions, regarded the Convention as
binding in perpetuity. . . . Whether the Convention of 1815

was or was not invalidated by the subsequent rebellion of
1817–18, what interpretation should properly be assigned to
the Proclamation of 1818 issued after the rebellion, whether
the recommendations of the Royal Commission of 1831–32
were or were not justified by the circumstances prevailing
at the time, and whether and how far the Report of this
Commission was framed with the concurrence and good will
of the Kandyans themselves, are all questions which we
must leave to the historian and the student". (Report of the
Donoughmore Commission, 1928.)

The wise historian or student is unlikely to rush in where
special commissioners fear to tread.

Brownrigg determined not to allow a recurrence of the
events of 1817–18. In future the Kandyan nobles were not to
be given authority which they could abuse. Kandyan provincial governors were again appointed, but this time without
their former power. Administration became the responsibility
of a small Board of Commissioners, under whom were eleven
district agents.

In 1820 Brownrigg left Ceylon and Sir Edward Paget succeeded him as governor. Paget was a professional soldier of
distinguished record, but his two years as Governor of Ceylon
were in no way remarkable and in 1823 he was appointed
Commissioner-in-Chief, East India. It was, however, during
his term of office that it was decided to send a special commission of inquiry to Ceylon and certain other British Colonies.
In July 1822, Mr. Robert Wilmot, Under-Secretary of State
for War and the Colonies (who, as Sir Robert Wilmot-Horton,
became Governor of Ceylon in 1831) proposed in the House
of Commons that a commission be set up to inquire into the
state of affairs in Ceylon, the Cape of Good Hope, and Mauritius,
and into the administration of justice in the Leeward Islands.
His proposal was supported by Wilberforce and Hume and
was accepted by the House.

Sir Edward Barnes became governor in place of Paget in
1824. Barnes was a professional soldier, and on one occasion
he proposed that the Ceylon civil service should be abolished
and the administration of the island entrusted to serving army

officers. He was a man of staunchly conservative views and was described by one of his subordinates as "paternal . . . more or less despotic . . . benevolent. . . . His government was characterized by its decision and great energy". His administration was notable for three things. First, his insistence that his senior officials should learn one of the native languages. Second, his encouragement of agriculture—and especially the coffee industry—and trade. Third, his continual emphasis on the need for good transport and communications in the island. He took the view that, from both the military and economic standpoints, the island needed a network of reliable roads and bridges, and he did not hesitate to resort to the traditional system of forced labour to achieve his end. In 1831 Barnes was appointed Commander-in-Chief, India, and Sir Robert Wilmot-Horton became governor.

*   *   *   *   *

Ceylon, during the third decade of the nineteenth century, had a population of just under a million, of whom about a quarter lived in the Kandyan provinces. The senior level of the civil service consisted of less than forty persons, ten of whom held military commissions and performed their civil duties in addition to serving their regiments. Appointments to the civil service were made by the governor. All power, executive and legislative, rested with the governor, who had the assistance of a small advisory council of officials appointed by him. He was not obliged to seek the advice of this council on any matter, nor if he did so was he bound to accept the advice he received.

The people as a whole were ignorant and poor. Wages varied between 6d. a day in Colombo and 3d. a day in the interior. The system of forced labour, which William Colebrooke was later to condemn so vigorously, operated unjustly. The people were conscripted for service, both paid and unpaid, of various kinds—the felling and dragging of timber, the construction of roads and bridges, the catching of elephants for public use, and the collection of cinnamon. There were additional free services which were required by travelling officials: coolies and porters had to be provided, food procured, rest houses covered with white cloth, the roads decorated with palm leaves, and torches carried before the distinguished traveller.

In addition to the system of forced labour for public works was the analogous system for religious ceremonies in Kandy. Much of the land of Ceylon belonged to Buddhist temples, and the tenants were required by the Buddhist authorities to render services and contributions of various kinds. This was an irksome irritation at its best, causing considerable hardship and distress at its worst. It necessitated long absences from home in order to render some trifling and formal service on odd occasions during a religious festival lasting several weeks.

Anxiety about conditions in Ceylon was increasing in London, and the Government's policy was discussed in the Press and Parliament. A typical debate took place in the House of Commons in May 1830. John Stewart complained of the high cost of administration, the restrictive fiscal arrangements, the government monopoly of cinnamon, the defective administration of justice, and the excessive size of the military establishment, adding that in his opinion a military officer made a bad governor and that it had been Ceylon's misfortune to have had a succession of governors who were military men. Daniel O'Connell complained of the treatment of the Catholic population. Joseph Hume, a persistent critic of British colonial policy, claimed that this was a case "crying for inquiry and reform". "Here is one of the finest colonies in the world," yet the revenue of £350,000 a year was not sufficient to cover the cost of administration. He complained of the high salaries paid to the governor and other officials. "If the shackles which now cramp industry and commercial enterprise were removed, and the establishment of the island put on a fair and liberal footing, the colony would pay all its expenses, and pay off its debts." Sir George Murray, Secretary of State for the Colonial and War Department, replied for the Government with a temporizing speech which reads very much like a departmental brief. He admitted that there had been "considerable difficulties" but suggested that the House would do well to wait for the report of the commission of inquiry.

The commission had been set up in 1823 and consisted of

John Thomas Bigge, William Blair, and Lt.-Col. (later Sir)
William M. G. Colebrooke. It was decided that judicial administration should be the subject of a separate inquiry, and
this was conducted by Charles Hay Cameron, an able jurist.
The commissioners visited the Cape and from there went to
Mauritius. Bigge and Blair both suffered from ill-health and
returned home, and Colebrooke arrived in Ceylon alone in
1829. He had been in Ceylon some years before as a young
officer, and had also served in India, Java, Sumatra, and the
Persian Gulf.

Though the whole burden of the inquiry fell on Colebrooke,
he was perfectly equal to the task and set about his work with
zeal and energy. He was a man of imagination and vision. He
prepared questionnaires which he circulated to persons of
importance in the island. He travelled widely, visiting almost
every part of the island. His conclusions were forthright and
his recommendations for the future bold. He did not accept
the opinions of others without testing them against his own
experience. His report was published in 1832 and was the
first attempt to produce a coherent plan for the administration
of the island.

After reviewing the system of government then in operation
he concluded that

"while it is free from some of the prominent objections to
those which have been adopted on the continent of India,
the general spirit and tendency of it has been unfavourable
to the improvement of the country. Some beneficial measures
have from time to time been adopted, but no regular control
has been exercised over the acts and proceedings of the
Governor, nor has his recognized responsibility for the
measures adopted by him on his own judgment been rendered
practically efficient. From the remoteness of the settlement,
the nature of the government, and the absence of all open
discussion of public affairs, the Governor has been almost
the exclusive organ through whom authentic information has
been derived, and with whom any measures of improvement
have originated. Without his co-operation no beneficial
change could be effected, and the inhabitants have been

accustomed to regard his authority as absolute. When un-popular measures have been enforced by him, they have usually remonstrated against them, and in some instances have resisted their operation.

As measures have been proposed and adopted without any previous notice, the people have had no opportunity of explaining their objection to the passing of regulations which have injuriously affected their interests. Besides the system of monopoly maintained, and in some cases extended, by the government, the power exercised by the Governor of regulating duties, and imposing taxes has been injurious to commerce and to the influx and accumulation of capital.

The claims which have been enforced by the government to the labour of the native inhabitants have been also very unfavourable to agricultural industry and improvement, except in cases where that labour has been applied in the repairs or execution of works required for the cultivation of rice. . . . These claims to public labour have given an interest to government in upholding the distinctions of caste, and the privileges of the headmen, through whom it has exercised an indefinite control over the people and their resources.

The maintenance of separate and independent establish-ment for the maritime and the Kandyan provinces has been impolitic, in the check it has opposed to that assimilation which is on every account desirable to promote between the various classes of whom the population is composed. By maintaining a separate government at Kandy, the influence of the chiefs has been upheld to the prejudice, in some instances, of the people."

Colebrooke's main proposals for reform were as follows:

1. Kandy should be incorporated into the general system of administration, and the island divided into five provinces, each under a Government Agent.

2. An Executive Council, consisting of half a dozen senior officials, should be set up to assist the governor in all matters connected with the raising or spending of public money. The council should have the right to call for information, and the

minutes of its proceedings should be transmitted to the Secretary of State.

3. A Legislative Council should be formed consisting of a number of senior officials, "provision being at once made for the admission of any respectable inhabitants, European or native". The council should have the right to call for information and to consider any matter submitted to it by the governor, any of its members, or by private individuals. Measures approved by the Council should be laid before the governor and, if passed by him, should become provisional laws pending the assent of His Majesty. In the case of measures approved by the Council and rejected by the governor and measures proposed by the governor and rejected by the Council, a full report of the matter should be sent to the Secretary of State and if these measures should be approved by His Majesty they should become law. Colebrooke maintained that

"the people are entitled to expect that their interests and wishes may be attended to, and their rights protected; and although the ignorance and prejudice which still prevail generally throughout the country may preclude the adoption of their views upon all subjects, it would be consistent with the policy of a liberal government that they should have an opportunity of freely communicating their opinions of the effects of the legislative changes that may be proposed. . . . Such a council is not proposed as an institution calculated in itself to provide effectually for the legislation of the island at a more advanced stage of its progress. It will, however, tend to remove some of the obstacles which have retarded [the] improvement. . . . The efficacy of the legislative council may be improved from time to time by the appointment to it of respectable and influential inhabitants. . . ."

4. The public service should be freely open to all persons, irrespective of race or caste, and "the means of education held out to the natives whereby they may in time qualify themselves for holding some of the higher appointments". Officials should be liable to suspension for misconduct but should not otherwise be removable by the governor as had previously been the

case. He recommended that substantial reductions be effected in official salaries, the saving amounting to over 20 per cent. He also recommended the abolition of a number of posts, including those of Commissioner of Revenue, Paymaster-General and Commissioner of Stamps, Private Secretary to the Governor, and eight of the magistrates.

5. Some of Colebrooke's most outspoken comments were reserved for the system of forced labour, and he recommended its complete abolition even if this meant—which he considered unlikely—that the government might in some cases be unable to secure the labour it required. The system of compulsory labour, he said, had been irregularly maintained and had produced much injustice.

6. Colebrooke recommended the ending of the government monopoly of the cinnamon industry. He regarded this monopoly as "oppressive and injurious". He also suggested that the government monopoly of salt ("injurious to the people in several respects") should be abolished.

7. Village headmen should be elected on a small property franchise, and should hold office for three years.

8. There should be a general codification of the laws and customs of the island. Much uncertainty and confusion had arisen in the administration of justice, and this could only be ended by the adoption of a comprehensive and consistent code of law and custom. All legal distinctions of race and caste should be abolished, and the new system should be directed towards "a gradual approximation to the principles of English law." Colebrooke gained the impression from the Kandyan chiefs that they would have no objection to the adoption of a general code which would apply equally to Kandy and the maritime provinces. This point is of some importance in view of later Kandyan complaints that Britain had violated the Convention of 1815 in applying to Kandy the general code of the island, without reference to Kandyan traditions and customs.

9. Colebrooke suggested that a uniform system of granting land to settlers should be adopted and that all discriminatory practices against non-Europeans should be abandoned.

10. Certain reforms in the educational system were also urged.

   Cameron's report on judicial procedure, which also appeared
in 1832, was much influenced by the advanced ideas of Jeremy
Bentham and was highly critical of the system of administering
justice in force in Ceylon at the time of his visit. He objected
to the fact that the judges were persons without legal training.
They were, he wrote, "gentlemen not only unconnected with
the profession of the law, but whose education has been in no
degree adapted to the special purpose of qualifying them for
the administration of justice". They were, moreover, "entirely
dependant upon the governor's pleasure for their continuance
in office. Not only can the governor displace them without
inquiry for alleged misconduct, but he can, without any harsh
exercise of authority, and consequently without any responsibility to public opinion, remove them to some other department. . . . The relation thus subsisting between the local judge
and the executive government is incompatible with a proper
degree of judicial independence".
   Cameron maintained the irreproachable principle that
justice should not be denied to any man because of his poverty.
He pointed out that this principle was not honoured in Ceylon,
since every step which a suitor took involved the payment of
stamp duty. "Those who cannot pay are plainly told that they
have no right by law to the services of a court of justice."
   Cameron was not blind to the difficulties in the way of
reform. "The disregard of an oath, and of truth in general
among the natives is notorious; not less so is their readiness
to gratify their malignant passions through the medium of
vexatious litigation." The government had tried to discourage
overmuch litigation by limiting the cases which could be the
subject of appeal. Certain cases involving disputes about
property, for instance, could only go to appeal courts if the
value involved exceeded £1 17s. 6d. Cameron questioned the
rightness of this regulation. He did not admit that all petty
litigation was evil nor that petty injustice could be prevented
or remedied any other way.

   "A suit for a sum under £1 17s. 6d. may indeed seem
an object of contempt to a European judge. Considering
any individual case by itself, he would probably rather pay

the amount claimed than be at the trouble of examining and deciding the question between the parties: but in the eyes of a native of Ceylon of the lower class, such a sum appears, and with great reason, an object of very high importance, an object, the unjust detention of which is calculated to excite in his mind the most violent animosity against the person who commits the wrong, and the government which fails to redress it.

Among all the duties incumbent on the British rulers in the East, it is impossible to name one more imperative than that of providing for the effectual decision by public authority of the disputes arising among the poorer classes. . . .

The misery and resentment of a poor man suffering under an act of injustice are most cruelly aggravated by the contempt with which the legislative and the judicial powers thus openly treat his misfortunes, and I can conceive no tie which will bind the lower people so strongly to their government, as a judicial establishment so conceived as that the very same attention and discrimination should be employed upon their causes as upon those of their affluent neighbours."

Cameron's proposals for judicial reform were as radical and far-reaching as Colebrooke's proposals in the administrative and financial sphere. They cannot be considered in detail here, but their result was to introduce a uniform system of justice based on sound ethical principles.

CHAPTER VIII

FROM THE COLEBROOKE COMMISSION TO LORD TORRINGTON'S ADMINISTRATION, 1833-50

Magnanimity in politics is not seldom the truest wisdom; and a great empire and little minds go ill together.—Edmund Burke, in the House of Commons, 22nd March, 1775.

THE recommendations of Colebrooke and Cameron were no doubt too advanced for their generation. The commissioners applied to the problems they encountered criteria which few would have questioned if applied to similar conditions in England but which were widely regarded as quite unsuited to the very different circumstances obtaining in Ceylon. Less than twenty years had elapsed since the barbarous practices of the King of Kandy had ended with his removal from the throne, and less than fifteen years since the Kandyan Revolt. The people as a whole were still backward and neither desired nor understood the principles of parliamentary democracy and impartial justice. These principles were, indeed, but imperfectly understood in Britain.

Nevertheless, the proposals of Colebrooke and Cameron, though visionary, were to have a profound influence not only in Ceylon but throughout the British Colonial Empire. The principles they advocated were subjected to fierce criticism at the time, but later generations came to accept them without question.

Sir Edward Barnes saw which way the wind was blowing and resigned in 1831. He had opposed the setting up of the commission of inquiry and disliked the way it had done its work. He thought the proposal to open the public service to Ceylonese "must ultimately lead to a separation of the island from British control. . . . I can only observe that at the present state of society the proposed measure is ludicrous enough, but what may be produced in time. . . . I will not pretend to try. But I have no hesitation in saying that black faces and white can never be so amalgamated together in society as to be on an equal footing: the one or the other must predominate". He regarded any form of popular government as "quite out of the question". "The people cannot nor ought to have under existing circumstances any greater share in the government than at present. . . . I should most decidedly object to a government composed of members associated with the governor and having the right even of deciding measures proposed by him, and still more so of originating measures in themselves, as such a form of government must lead to discussion and I hold it to be a maxim of government that the executive authority should never be engaged in personal discussions." One of his colleagues wrote that representative government "cannot be seriously advocated by parties possessing a knowledge of the country, which is utterly deficient of the requisite elements of such a system. . . . A paternal form of government is the only one at present suited to the country".

Barnes's successor, Sir Robert Wilmot-Horton, was a man of liberal views and had both administrative and political experience. He had served in the House of Commons from 1812–30, and had for a time been Parliamentary Under-Secretary of State for War and the Colonies. He was, however, soon expressing his opposition to Colebrooke's proposals. He described them as "crude and impractical". He told the Secretary of State that he had come to the conclusion that Colebrooke's knowledge of Ceylon was superficial. He produced evidence from his own officials which cast doubt on the methods used by Colebrooke to collect evidence. He was opposed to the entry of Ceylonese into the public service and of their inclusion in the legislative council. "I know not a single high situation held by a member of the Civil Service, which is an object of ambition to any native, nor do I know any native calculated to execute the duties of such a situation, or whose appointment would give confidence to his fellow-countrymen." He also opposed the proposal to include unofficial Europeans in the legislative council. The merchants,

he wrote "are not merchants in the due sense of that word—
they have no local interest in the colony—they have no property
in it—they are mere agents for foreign houses". He deplored
the proposed reductions in salary for officials, believing that
this change would end the integrity of the public service.
"We had an active and energetic class of Public Servant. . . . We
have now, God knows, and I fear shall continue to have,
a mortified and dispirited set, in whose minds hope is
extinguished."

Nevertheless, the majority of Colebrooke's recommendations were put into force in 1832–3. An executive council,
consisting of five senior officials, was created. The governor
retained the right to reject the council's views provided that
he furnished the Secretary of State with a full report of the
matter. A legislative council was also created, consisting initially
of the governor and nine officials. In 1837 two English-speaking
unofficial members, nominated by the governor, were added:
and in 1845 the number of nominated unofficial members was
increased to six—one Tamil, one Low Country Sinhalese, one
Burgher, and three Europeans. 'Service Tenure' and forced
labour were abolished. The government monopoly of cinnamon
and other commodities was ended.

It was, however, the reform of the civil service which
created the greatest difficulties. Colebrooke had recommended
sweeping reductions in salaries, the abolition of a number of
posts, and the ending of the system of pensions. The salary
reductions varied in amount—that of the Treasurer was reduced from £2,000 a year to £1,500, for example, that of the
Collector of Customs from £1,574 to £1,000, that of the
Assistant Agent of the Seven Korales from £1,000 to £400.
Among the posts abolished were those of Commissioner of
Revenue and Paymaster-General. The British Treasury was,
of course, glad of the opportunity of reducing the cost of the
administration of Ceylon, but it was a short-sighted policy.
However good Colebrooke's other proposals might have been,
they could hardly have been regarded with favour by those
whose responsibility it was to put them into effect if the
salaries of those persons had just been substantially reduced.
And not only did this step create hostility among the existing

officials; it also had the effect of deterring able people from entering the service. Much of Maitland's good work was undone by the change.

At the same time that Wilmot-Horton was struggling to prevent the application of Colebrooke's proposals for the civil service, he was engaged in an unedifying dispute with the European community over the composition of the new legislative council. This body was to consist of the governor, nine officials, and six unofficial members nominated by the governor "as far as possible in equal proportions from the respectable European merchants or inhabitants and the higher classes of natives". Wilmot-Horton was unable to find suitably qualified unofficial persons to serve on the council, and twelve years were to elapse before the six appointments were made. The European merchants complained that the absence of the unofficial members was illegal and the acts of the council invalid. In fact the quorum of the council had been fixed at seven so that its proceedings could be perfectly legal in the absence of unofficial members.

* * * * *

For more than a decade following the publication of the reports of Colebrooke and Cameron, Ceylon was in the doldrums. The unwise changes, such as those relating to the civil service, were having a disastrous effect: the changes which were in themselves of a progressive nature were still in the experimental stage. During the early 1840s, when Sir Colin Campbell was governor and Lord Stanley (afterwards Earl of Derby) was Secretary of State, there was a slight improvement. Soon after assuming the governorship, Campbell sent a series of dispatches to London on conditions in the island. The quality of the civil service, he wrote, was steadily deteriorating: it was quite impossible to find able persons to fill the vacancies as they arose. The principle of promotion by seniority rather than ability meant that a high proportion of the officials were filling posts for which they were patently unqualified. The auditor, according to Campbell, would have made a good treasurer, the treasurer a good auditor. Each time a vacancy in the service occurred it was necessary to make as many as fifteen changes so that each official moved to a more senior post.

Stanley was, indeed, shocked by the state of the civil service. "I find a most unhappy unanimity as to the low state of public feeling which has of late years crept in among the junior members of the Civil Service," he wrote, "—their want of energy and proper pride, and their indifference to improvement. They are represented as listless in the discharge of their functions—contented with the bare performance of those duties which can be exacted from them—and wanting in the zeal without which their services cannot be advantageous."

Stanley decided that the only solution was "to revert in a considerable measure to the system existing previously to 1832". The salary cuts were largely restored, pensions reintroduced, and promotion by seniority abandoned. "No individual whatever his length of service should be entitled to promotion unless he should be not only competent, but the most competent person whom the Civil Service might offer."

The regulations relating to the learning of native languages were also tightened up. In 1822 Barnes had introduced the principle that only those officials who had passed an examination in a native language could be promoted to a senior post, but the regulation had in practice been ignored. Stanley ordered that the rule should be strictly applied.

One important change was made over a matter which had arisen directly from the low salaries paid to civil servants. Officials had for long been forbidden to engage in trade but were allowed to own land and sell the produce. This seemed an innocent enough regulation at first, but soon the civil servants were spending so much time supervising their own coffee plantations that their official work was neglected. Campbell regarded the practice as demoralizing, and on his advice Lord Stanley gave instructions that it should cease. The order was notified in the following terms:

> "His Lordship has directed, that it be distinctly understood that no civil servant will be permitted to engage in any agricultural or commercial pursuits for the sake of profit; and that all who may have done so must, within a reasonable

time, dispose of their property, or retire from the public
service; and that this rule be fully and promptly carried into
effect; the penalty of any evasion of the *bona fide* compliance
with this rule will be immediate dismissal."

This decision led, not unexpectedly, to considerable opposition and criticism from those whose interests were affected.
The civil servants complained "that Her Majesty's Government in the first instance, encouraged agricultural undertakings
by civil servants; that it has throughout been aware that they
were so engaged . . . and that the governors of the colony
have, in more than one instance, been themselves participators
in them". They objected to the inevitable financial loss they
would suffer. The knowledge that the sale of so much property
was to take place would depreciate the value of the estates.
They asked for an extension of the period which had been
allowed for compliance with the order.

Henry Tufnell, the Whig Member for Devonport, in raising
the matter in the House of Commons at Westminster, emphasized that the practice had begun with the "warmest approba-
tion" of successive governors, and complained of the limited
time allowed for giving effect to the new ruling. But his main
criticism of the government related to the publication by the
governor of Lord Stanley's outspoken views of the civil service. Lord Stanley's censure, though undoubtedly deserved,
was described by Tufnell as "a most decided and uncalled-for
insult".

In the end Stanley modified his original instructions. He
was adamant that no civil servant should in future buy land.
Those, however, who owned land prior to the publication of
the order might retain it so long as they did not themselves
superintend its cultivation and so long as the possession of the
land did not interfere with the performance of their official
duties.

*   *   *   *   *

So far in this chapter we have been concerned with administrative matters and in particular with the civil service. We

must now turn to the people of Ceylon and consider in what way their conditions of life had been changing. The low standards of efficiency and conduct in the civil service were matched by the misery and ignorance of the people. The population in the year 1845 stood at about a million and a half compared with just under a million in 1830. Plantation labourers from South India were reaching Ceylon at a rate of about 2,500 a year.

There had been a great increase in intemperance and drunkenness, and this in turn led to banditry and other criminal activities. Reference has already been made in discussing the recommendations of Colebrooke and Cameron to the people's love of litigation. This had not only increased in extent but had also been accompanied by an unprecedented amount of corruption and perjury.

Irrigation was neglected. Whereas formerly the government had done a good deal to encourage native agriculture it had latterly devoted its main energies to looking after the interests of European planters and merchants. Disease and drought were having a disastrous effect on the peasantry. The development of coffee plantations by Europeans was unsettling: Low Country Sinhalese flocked to the interior to do work in connection with the plantations which the Kandyans lacked the experience to undertake.

Dissatisfaction was not, however, confined to the native communities. Memorials, petitions, declarations and similar documents from the European merchants in Colombo demanded various reforms. It was urged that the Legislative Council be reconstituted so that it included more unofficial members, and that it be given greater powers; that the large proportion of the Ceylon revenue devoted to military purposes should be reduced; that the roads in the island should be repaired; that the British import duty on Ceylon coffee be reduced.

Those who knew Ceylon realized that trouble was brewing. In May 1847 Viscount Torrington assumed office as governor and was almost immediately at loggerheads with all unofficial groups in the island. By the middle of 1848 Ceylon was troubled with the most serious disturbances that had occurred since the Kandyan Revolt thirty years earlier.

The rising of 1848 was preceded by a dispute which, though minor in itself, symbolized the growing breach between government and people. The so-called Veranda Question had arisen over a long-standing rule that verandas in Colombo should not be allowed to encroach on public thoroughfares. The rule had not been strictly enforced, but early in 1846 it became necessary to widen some of the streets. Sir Colin Campbell had ordered that all verandas which formed an obstruction were to be removed. All other verandas could become the legal property of the owner by purchasing from the government the land on which they were situated. The price was originally fixed in April at from 9d. to 2s. 6d. per square foot depending on the situation, was reduced to from 6d. to 1s. 6d. per square foot in August, and finally to from 3d. to 9d. per square foot in October.

The dispute dragged on, and in 1847, after Torrington had become governor, Earl Grey, Secretary of State for War and the Colonies, advised that the regulation should be modified. In June, within a few weeks of his arrival in Ceylon, Torrington received a deputation of inhabitants of Colombo and treated them extremely discourteously. He determined to adhere strictly to the original regulation, and wrote to Grey to that effect. He had his way, but only at the cost of making many enemies among all communities in Ceylon.

There had been minor disturbances in Kandy in 1842 and 1843. In 1842, as in 1818, a man claiming to be the king had established himself in the jungle with a handful of followers. Meetings were held at night at which the pretender told the villagers that he had dreamed of driving out the English. The pretender was arrested and sentenced to fourteen years hard labour in chains. The associates of the pretender were acquitted. In 1843 a similar outbreak occurred.

The rising of 1848 was not wholly unexpected except, perhaps, by Torrington himself. Major Thomas Skinner, the Commissioner of Roads, had told Torrington on the latter's arrival in Ceylon that the disorganization in parts of Kandy must inevitably end in anarchy if steps were not taken to remedy the situation. Torrington seems to have taken little heed of this advice. He described the rising in a letter to Earl

H

Grey, the Secretary of State, as "unforeseen". He asked for special funds to cover the cost of suppressing the rising, and emphasized that the explosion "must be principally attributed to the policy long pursued to the Kandyan people before I arrived in the country". This statement was undoubtedly true: Major Skinner supported this view, holding that Torrington "could hardly be held responsible for a social disorganization which had its origin long antecedent to his assuming the government". But it exemplified Torrington's ineffectual approach to the complex problems with which he was faced. It was typical of Torrington to ascribe all the blame for the disturbances to events beyond his control.

The first news of trouble to reach Torrington came at the end of June 1848 in a letter from the Superintendent of Police at Kandy. A police sergeant had reported "that there is a talk around the country of a certain person pretending himself to be a prince, or some high authority, exciting the common people to acts of insubordination". The police superintendent commented: "I am quite confident that no serious disturbance or insurrection will take place."

A week after this letter was written, a large unarmed crowd (estimated to number between 3,000 and 4,000) gathered in Kandy and complained of certain new taxes which had recently been imposed. The Government Agent tried unsuccessfully to address the gathering, and when it seemed to him likely to get out of control, he called on the military to disperse the crowd. Two days later Sir Emerson Tennent, the Colonial Secretary, received a number of deputations in Kandy and discussed the grievances. The conference passed off without incident. The situation seemed to have returned to normal, and Torrington wrote to Grey on 9th July: "I do not apprehend any disturbance or any further renewal of the excitement." Three days later, in a further report to the Secretary of State, Torrington wrote:

"According to the most recent account received from Kandy this morning tranquillity continued to prevail. . . . The interview of the several deputations of the people from the neighbourhood with the Colonial Secretary on Saturday last, the 8th, has been followed by the happiest results.

Nothing could be more successful than the candid explanation offered to them of the errors into which they had been
led by a few discontented persons who had purposely misled
the people."

On 25th July, about three weeks after the original disturbances, the police superintendent at Kandy informed Torrington of reports he had received of large armed crowds
gathering for the purpose of creating alarm, but offered his
opinion that "one-half of these reports are unfounded".

The following day (26th July) there was a minor disturbance at Colombo and the crowd was only prevented from
getting out of hand by the intervention of the military. The
ringleader was the editor of the Colombo *Observer*, a certain
Dr. Christopher Elliott, a European physician who had lived
in Ceylon for fourteen years. Torrington was much upset that
"one or two turbulent Europeans, supported and assisted by
many of the peculiar class of people called Burghers" seemed
to be encouraging the feeling of dissatisfaction among the
Ceylonese. He emphasized in dispatches to Grey his determination to show firmness and "resist to the utmost these
insidious attempts to pervert the native mind". He spoke of
the need to use "the strong arm of power", "a rigorous hand",
and "the severity of justice". He also gave his opinion that the
disturbances at Kandy and Colombo were totally unconnected.

On the day on which the Colombo disturbances took place,
the pretender to the Kandyan throne was crowned in a temple
in the interior. This was the signal for general revolt in Kandy.
There were several armed clashes between the government
forces and the rebels, and a number of rebel leaders were
captured, court-martialled, and shot. It was not until the end
of September that the pretender was captured. He was tried
later in the year and sentenced to death, the judge recommend-
ing that the sentence should be commuted to some lesser punishment. Torrington agreed to this course and informed Grey
that he had commuted the sentence to transportation for life:
"and by way of making a more lasting impression upon the
minds of the Kandians, I propose that their pretended king
shall receive a severe public flogging at Kandy preparatory to

transportation". In Kandy during the period of martial law, 29th July to 10th October, eighteen persons were condemned to death, twenty-eight to transportation, and sixty-six to other forms of punishment (usually fifty lashes and a period of imprisonment with hard labour).

These severe measures led to widespread criticism in both Ceylon and England. Torrington's conduct was roundly condemned in the British Press. One paper asserted that "more intolerable grievances were never sustained by a loyal people than those inflicted upon the Kandians at the time of their revolt". Another paper wrote that "a total disregard of justice and of mercy" had characterized Torrington's conduct. A motion for the appointment of a Select Committee was passed by the House of Commons in February 1849 after a series of revelations which did little credit to Torrington's administration. H. J. Baillie led the attack and accused the government of "tyranny and repression". He said that under the system of government in Ceylon ("pure and simple despotism") discontent among the native population could only lead to open rebellion. Joseph Hume demanded the recall of Lord Torrington and the resignation of Earl Grey. Peel felt that Torrington had gone too far, especially in ordering that the pretender to the Kandyan throne should be publicly flogged, and in insisting that a Buddhist priest who had been condemned to death should be executed in the full canonical robes of his order. Disraeli said that Lord Torrington's only qualification for the office of governor seemed to be that he had been a director of a railway company. Adderley, on the other hand, suggested that Torrington's sole qualification was that "he had administered a farm in Kent".

Lord John Russell, the Prime Minister, put in a half-hearted defence of Torrington and Grey, but admitted that the suppression of the rebellion had been a little drastic. He confessed that there was insufficient justification for the atrocities mentioned by Peel. Henry Labouchere, the President of the Board of Trade, and Benjamin Hawes, Under-Secretary for the Colonies, both spoke loyally in defence of Grey and Torrington.

The Select Committee was a strong one, its members including Baillie, Hume, Peel, Gladstone, Disraeli, Charles Viliers, C. B. Adderley, and Stuart Wortley. The government persistently obstructed its work. They suppressed relevant information, put difficulties in the way of securing documents and witnesses, and tried to prevent the publication of the evidence taken before the committee. Much of the evidence revealed to the committee was damaging to Torrington. One witness reported him as saying of a certain priest who was executed on 26th August, 1848: "By God, if all the proctors in the place said that man was innocent, he should be shot tomorrow morning."

Finally, in 1851, a motion to the effect that the measures taken to suppress the revolt were "excessive and uncalled for" was debated in the House of Commons and defeated by 282 votes to 202, Disraeli and Gladstone being among those who voted with the minority.

Torrington justified his conduct with vigour. The Kandyans, he said, "were astonished at nothing so much as the leniency and the forbearance of the government". On his return to England he defended his actions in the House of Lords. He had, he said, endeavoured honestly and conscientiously to fulfill his duty. He had always acted with the concurrence of his executive and legislative councils, and in military matters had consulted the officers most competent to give advice. The rebellion was "most serious and most dangerous". With regard to the execution of a priest in his sacerdotal dress, Torrington said that "this man had no other dress. . . . Had he not been executed in that garment, he would have been executed naked". In any case it was necessary "to make an example of him", to demonstrate that "priestly character and robes did not confer any exemption from the consequences of such grave crimes". He asked the House to consider the difficult position in which he was placed and he repeated that he had done his duty to the best of his ability.

The causes of the revolt were complex, and in the pages that follow some of the main causes will be given in the words of some of the witnesses who appeared before the Select Committee.

1. *General dissatisfaction.* "There had been a general dissatisfaction on the part of the community in general with the

existing government." (George Ackland, merchant.) "Among the headmen generally of the maritime provinces I think there exists a feeling of dissatisfaction and want of confidence in the present government" (Henry Lewis Layard, merchant and planter). "The whole system of colonial administration might be revised with great advantage" (Philip Anstruther, Colonial Secretary of Ceylon, 1830-45). "The great evil of which we have to complain is the disorganization from the want of proper government in the rural districts" (Major Thomas Skinner, Commissioner of Roads in Ceylon). "Nothing has given me more discouragement in Ceylon than the reluctance which I have found among the civil servants to adopt measures of improvement. . . . The general character of the service is apathy, approaching almost to indifference" (Sir Emerson Tennent, Colonial Secretary of Ceylon).

2. *Government and officials out of touch with native opinion.* "One of the greatest evils of our government has been the want of intercourse, and of sympathy with the natives, on the part of the civil functionaries. . . . I attribute the retrograde feeling of the population generally, in the first place, to go to the fountain head, to a want of knowledge of the country on the part of its governors" (Skinner). "There is a complete curtain drawn in Ceylon between the government and the governed; no person connected with the government under-stands the language; very few of them have the remotest idea of the customs of the natives; they are perfectly ignorant of the people. . . . Hardly any of the public servants can speak the language" (Anstruther). "Some government officers have almost entirely ceased to visit their own districts in person. . . . I have myself visited districts in the island in which an European had not been seen for thirty years" (Tennent).

3. *Headmen and priests.* "That the priests almost universally were implicated in this conspiracy, and connected with the arrangement of measures for its development, no one in Ceylon entertains a doubt" (Tennent). "One main reason why any cause of dissatisfaction might be exaggerated and rendered sufficient to excite the people to rebellion on the late occasion was that not only the chieftains who exercise influence over their dependents, and over the people at large, did all they

possibly could to incite them to rebellion on this occasion, but also that there was an exceedingly great disposition on the part of the whole of the Buddhist priests in the country to support the chiefs" (Sir T. Herbert Maddock, Indian Civil Service). "I think it [the rebellion] was entirely under the influence of the priests and the headmen. . . . The greatest misrepresentations were circulated in the country" (The Hon. Gerald Talbot, Ceylon Civil Service). "I think the cause of the headmen being dissatisfied arises principally from the abolition of compulsory labour" (Ackland). "In destroying, or allowing to be destroyed, the influence and authority of the chiefs, we unfortunately have not substituted any improved authority of our own. . . . The effect of this loss of authority . . . has been to throw whole districts, in fact almost all the rural population, into a state of disorganization" (Skinner). "The next cause [of the rebellion] was the growing indifference of the people to Buddhism, and to temple worship; and, it is more than probable, the means used by the priests to recover their lost influence, by disseminating rumours prejudicial to British rule" (Layard). "The priesthood have found their influence over the natives lessened by the advance of civilization" (Ackland).

4. *European encroachments.* "The native was discontented with the Europeans coming and settling down, because they required him to keep his cattle in their proper places, and not allow them to stroll about. . . . They also complained that their grazing lands were claimed by the government, and that they attributed to the coffee planters making their applications to purchase land" (Ackland). "The causes [of the disturbances] were in the first instance the encroachment by the Europeans, as well as by the government, upon the lands and forests. . . . Those lands became proscribed to a considerable extent by the claim of the government to the lands, and ultimate sale to the Europeans" (Layard). "The causes [of the general impatience which exists in the minds of all Kandyans] . . . are in a great degree to be traced to the operations of coffee planting and the introduction not only of Europeans as settlers in the midst of their hills and forests, but likewise to that which has given them much greater offence, viz. the introduction of Malabar coolies, who came there in search of labour" (Tennent).

5. *Legislative Council.* "The greater portion of the Europeans are rather inclined to giving the natives some voice in the election of members of the Legislative Council, to take the power of nomination away from the governor, in fact" (Talbot). "My opinion with regard to the Legislative Council is, that the unofficial members should be equal in number to the official members" (Frederick Saunders, Collector of Customs). "I think it is necessary that the Legislative Council should be remodelled; the Legislative Council, as representing the people, in some way or other should, I think, have a voice in the administration of the funds and the revenue" (Layard).

6. *Taxes.* "The third cause [of the disturbances] is the enactment of a series of taxes opposed to the prejudices and habits of the people, and the enforcement of which first gave rise to a demonstration of discontent, and subsequently to the rebellion and disorder which ensued" (Layard). "I think, unquestionably, the taxes led to the riots in this way: in all former instances the discontent was on the part of the chiefs . . . but those taxes, for the first time, have rendered the lower classes discontented" (Anstruther). "I think direct taxes are altogether objectionable in Ceylon; the natives have never been accustomed to them" (Sanders). "The natives, seeing so many taxes all brought in at one time, made use of that argument to show that it was the intention of the government to tax everything" (Ackland). "The leaders of the mob who were present at Martelle were always talking to the people about the taxes" (Henry Collingwood Selby, Queen's Advocate, Ceylon).

CHAPTER IX

DEVELOPMENT, 1850-77

*There is pain in acquiring wealth, pain in preserving
what has been acquired, pain in its loss, and pain in its
expenditure.*—Sanskrit proverb.

THE disturbances of 1848 represented the last serious attempt
on the part of the Ceylonese to end British rule by force. The
harsh repressive measures of Lord Torrington had created
such an uproar in the United Kingdom that he was recalled in
1850. He retired to the obscurity of the post of Lord-in-Waiting,
for six years to the Prince Consort and then for twenty-five
years to Queen Victoria. Sir Emerson Tennent, the Chief
Secretary, was dismissed from the Ceylon Civil Service, and
spent much of his time during the next few years writing a
remarkable book on Ceylon which remains a standard work to
this day. Philip Wodehouse, another civil servant, also left
Ceylon, though he later became governor successively of
British Honduras, British Guiana, Cape Colony, and Bombay.

Torrington's successor, Sir George William Anderson, had
served for more than forty years in the Indian Civil Service,
and to him fell the task of restoring an atmosphere of confidence. The rigorous parliamentary inquiry in London had
created dissension within the civil service and led to much
uncertainty and lack of confidence. The Ceylonese were bitter
at the harshness of Torrington and his colleagues, and looked
to the future with apprehension. The finances of the island
were in a bad state, for the disturbances of 1848 had
coincided with a serious financial crisis which we must now
examine.

The Dutch had grown small quantities of coffee in Ceylon,
but its production had never been taken seriously and almost
ceased during the first years of British rule. Attempts were
made during the 1820s to revive the cultivation of coffee, and

113

a number of government plantations were opened. In order to stimulate production Sir Edward Barnes exempted the plantations from land tax and abolished the export duty. Coffee exports to the United Kingdom were, however, hampered by the discriminatory import duty—6d. per lb. on West Indian coffee and 9d. per lb. on all other coffee. In 1835 the duty on Ceylon coffee was fixed at 6d. per lb., and immediately production in Ceylon increased. Whereas in 1830 some 20,000 cwt. of coffee were being exported every year, the figure had risen to nearly 200,000 cwt. in 1845. An indication of the interest in coffee cultivation can be seen from the fact that in 1835 some 400 acres of crown land were sold to planters: six years later the figure was 78,685 acres.

The mania to own land in Ceylon and grow coffee was soon out of hand.

"The first ardent adventurers," wrote Sir Emerson Tennent, "pioneered the way through pathless woods, and lived for months in log huts. . . . The new life in the jungle was full of excitement and romance. . . . So dazzling was the prospect that expenditure was unlimited; and its profusion was only equalled by the ignorance and inexperience of those to whom it was entrusted. . . . In the midst of these visions of riches, a crash suddenly came which awoke the victims to the reality of ruin. The financial explosion of 1845 in Great Britain speedily extended its destructive influence to Ceylon; remittances ceased, prices fell, credit failed. . . . The consternation thus produced in Ceylon was proportionate to the extravagance of the hopes that were blasted; estates were forced into the market, and madly sold off for a twentieth part of the outlay incurred in forming them."

A colleague of Tennent wrote of the influx of European planters:

"Amongst these were not a few whose habits and conduct tended much to diminish the respect in which the English character had previously been held by the natives; while a most fatal error committed by the government,

in allowing its servants to embark in the seductive specula-
tion of coffee . . . weakened the moral influence which
they previously possessed, no less than it tended to cir-
cumscribe their pecuniary means of independence and
usefulness, and finally, in too many instances, ruined
their finances. It also placed their interests in rivalry with
their duty."

A coffee planter of experience gave three reasons for the
crisis: "first, the high rate of wages—secondly, the want of a
regular and abundant supply of labour—thirdly, the great
expense of transport from want of good roads." To illustrate
the extent of the disaster he quoted the case of "an estate that
was sold in 1843 for £15,000 was knocked down for £440
only". An article in the *Calcutta Review* instanced the case of
two estates which had cost £10,000 and were sold for £350.
At the same time, to complicate the situation, the price of
coffee was falling in London. From 120s. per cwt. in 1840 it
fell to as low as 27s. in 1849.

The coffee planters constantly complained of the slowness
with which new roads were constructed. Barnes had made a
start with building a network of roads, using forced labour.
Colombo was linked to Kandy with a reasonably good road
which was extended part of the way towards Trincomalee.
Another road was built from Colombo to Galle and some
distance beyond. Forced labour was abolished after the publication of the Colebrooke Report, but Wilmot-Horton managed
to get some additional roads built in spite of Treasury
complaints of extravagance. The road from Kandy to Trincomalee was completed. Kandy was also linked both to
Puttalam and to Jaffna. Anderson, Torrington's successor, was
especially criticized by the Europeans for his failure to build
new roads or repair old ones. His difficulties were certainly
great and it was manifestly impossible for him to embark on
lavish expenditure on public works. He did, in fact, do more
to keep the roads in repair than his critics were prepared to
admit.

*   *   *   *   *

Another problem with which Anderson had to deal concerned the policy of the government towards the Buddhist religion. The Sinhalese were, and still are, mainly Buddhist and the Sinhalese were, of course, the most numerous community in the island. Buddhism had been the state religion of Kandy, and the king had been not only a secular ruler but had performed important religious functions. The Convention of 1815 declared that the Buddhist religion was to be "inviolable, and its Rites, Ministers and Places of worship are to be maintained and protected". What this declaration meant was never clear: one view was that "in the practical working out of the Convention the British Sovereign succeeded to all the rights and obligations of the Kandyan King in respect of the Buddhist Church". Brownrigg himself wrote to the Secretary of State about the meaning of the word 'inviolable'. "In Cingalese the expression is literally 'cannot be broken down'."

"I greatly lament," he wrote, "that anything under my sanction should have generated even a momentary idea, that I could possibly have overlooked or neglected the strong and reiterated injunctions by which the dissemination of Christian knowledge is recommended to my support. . . . I think it requires no great foresight to predict that the gloom of ignorance and superstition which has hitherto enveloped that unfortunate region will at no distant period be materially dissipated by the gradual and insensible diffusion of religious knowledge."

The Proclamation of 1818 declared that Buddhist priests and ceremonies should "receive the respect which in former times was shown them", and there was a further guarantee of "the peaceable exercise by all other persons of the religion which they respectively profess".

There was a good deal of opposition in England to the apparently close association of the Ceylon Government with the Buddhist religion. It was argued that Britain was a Christian country and should use its influence overseas to extend the Christian Church, not to protect and maintain a pagan religion. In 1844 Lord Stanley informed the governor that the time had arrived "when the British Government may, without breach of faith, and without risk to the tranquility of the colony, relieve itself from all connection with idolatry". In future the governor would have no responsibility for the appointment of priests, there would be no subsidy or grant to the Buddhist Church, the sacred Buddha's Tooth would be entrusted to the care of priests, and so on. The difficulty about this policy was that it was withdrawing one arrangement without putting anything in its place. Campbell proposed a compromise which was approved by his Legislative Council, but this was rejected by Grey who had succeeded Stanley as Secretary of State. Grey regretted that he differed from the members of the Legislative Council in Ceylon but maintained that "the present is a case in which the principles brought into debate depend, not upon any local circumstances, but upon considerations which can be appreciated with equal clearness in whatever country they may be discussed, or which (it may be no exaggeration to say) can be appreciated more clearly at a distance from the scene of action".

Torrington examined the whole matter thoroughly and came to the view that the best method would be for the priests to elect their own officers, and for the Ceylon Government to give legal validity to the regulations for election by issuing a brief confirmatory ordinance. "Without legislative assistance of some kind. . . . I do not perceive how anarchy can be avoided." Grey, however, was adamant and refused to approve an arrangement of that sort.

This was the situation which Anderson found, and he quickly came to the view that the formal warrants appointing chief priests should be signed by the governor. Grey hesitatingly agreed to this course as he could see no alternative. Anderson was supported by the Bishop of Colombo, but there was a large and vocal opposition which included many of the clergy in Ceylon and was vigorously led by Dr. Elliott.

It was, perhaps, surprising that nobody thought of the obvious arrangement until a year later. Grey proposed that the chief priests should be elected by the priests of the temple, and that the governor should issue, not a certificate of appointment, but a certificate merely recognizing that the election had taken place and that the appointment had been made. This plan was apparently acceptable and Anderson's difficulties were at an end.

*   *   *   *   *

In 1855 Sir Henry Ward became governor. Ward had been a member of the diplomatic service for some years and had served in the House of Commons as a Liberal from 1832–49. He was a popular governor, but during his period of office determined attempts were made by the unofficial elements to secure a reform of the constitution. There had been no constitutional reforms since the recommendations of the Colebrooke Report were given effect. In fact, "between 1834 and the end of the first decade of the twentieth century there had ... been no important constitutional changes" (Report of the Donoughmore Commission, 1928).

The Legislative Council when Ward took office consisted of the governor, nine officials, and six unofficial members chosen by the governor. The criticisms of the constitution made by educated people in Ceylon were four in number.

First, that officials were in a majority in the Legislative Council. This meant that the governor could carry any measure on which he was determined by his control of the votes of the officials. The Colonial Office had laid it down that in the ordinary way the official members should be free to speak and vote in the council as they thought fit, but that in cases of importance the governor should have the power to require the resignation of, or to suspend, any official who was unwilling to support him. The result was that the *ultima ratio* was the governor's power to dismiss a recalcitrant official, and there were few who could afford to carry their opposition to gubernatorial policies to the extent of throwing up their jobs.

The demand for popular control of the Legislative Council was led by Dr. Elliott, the editor of the Colombo *Observer*, and was supported by the majority of Burghers. Ward described the Burghers as "the brazen wheels which, hidden from light, keep the golden hands of government in motion", but he considered that they possessed "neither the respect nor the affection

of the natives . . . if you value the peace of Ceylon you must
never give these gentlemen a preponderance in the Legislative
Council". He was, indeed, opposed to any idea of popular
government. "In a Colony the population of which consists
of seven or eight thousand European settlers, a small though
intelligent class of Burghers, and two million of Cingalese,
Tamils and Moormen, wholly unaccustomed to the working
of a constitutional system, you cannot introduce the principle
of Representative and Responsible Government . . . the Crown
for many years must hold the balance between European and
native interests."

The second criticism of the constitution was that the unofficial members of the Legislative Council were nominated
by the governor rather than elected. Elliott urged that the
natives should be allowed to elect the unofficial members of
the council. In the circumstances of the time this was an un-
realistic demand, but Ward made a slight concession towards
the principle of election when he permitted the Chamber of
Commerce and the Planters' Association to select two of the
three unofficial European members of the council.

The third criticism was that the Ceylonese were insuffici-
ently represented in the council. It was argued that a ratio of
three Ceylonese to thirteen Europeans (of whom ten were
government officials) meant that in any clash of interests the
European view would always prevail, and further that the three
Ceylonese chosen by the governor were not necessarily the
persons best able to defend Ceylonese interests. It was not,
however, until 1889 that Ceylonese representation was increased,
and then only to five in a council of eighteen members.

The fourth criticism was that the council possessed only
advisory functions. Although it was called a Legislative Council,
it was powerless to legislate if the governor wished otherwise.
It was a forum where grievances could be ventilated, and it had
a certain moral authority. But from a strictly legalistic point
of view it had little power. The governor had the right to veto
any ordinance passed by the council.

One of the reasons why the Europeans wanted a greater
voice in the conduct of affairs was the desire to secure by
legislation more and better communications to facilitate the

export of coffee. The revival of this industry had begun just before Ward's arrival in Ceylon, and the greatly increased revenue enabled the government to improve the communications system. About one million pounds were spent on the roads while Ward was governor. A start was also made on the construction of a railway line from Colombo to Kandy.

The story of the construction of the Colombo–Kandy line deserves a fuller treatment than can be given in this book. Work began in 1858, the estimated cost being just over £800,000. It was soon clear that this figure was little more than an extremely bad guess. The chief engineer in charge of construction thought it would cost over £2,200,000. This caused a stir and work was abandoned. It was restarted in 1863, great economy being exercised. The final cost came to about £1,750,000.

Besides his interest in improving the roads and in the construction of the Colombo–Kandy line, Ward also did a good deal to improve the irrigation system. He recognized that no prosperity for European planters and merchants would endure unless the native cultivators were prosperous. Agriculture had been neglected during centuries of civil war and foreign conquest. The people, wrote a British governor about this time, "were all emaciated, miserable, half-starved, and dejected-looking wretches. . . . They were dying out by disease and starvation; the embankment of their tanks had given way almost universally, and they had neither numbers nor co-operation nor vitality to repair them properly. The consequence was that the rice crops were most precarious, more often a failure than otherwise, and the wretched people lived on roots or cut down the forest, thereby doing enormous injury". Though formerly self-supporting Ceylon was now dependent for part of its food supply on imported rice. The extensive irrigation works of the early Sinhalese kings had fallen into disuse. "The large canals," wrote Ward, "have for centuries been out of use, and are only traceable by the remnants of their vast embankments." The few that had been maintained in use were "in a most dilapidated condition, and hastily and imperfectly patched up; seldom or never cleared. . . . A masonry sluice is a thing unknown, and each cultivator cuts a hole in the banks wherever it suits him when he wants water for his field".

Ward tackled the problem in an imaginative way. Instead of making the government alone responsible for irrigation, he revived the old system of village councils. This system of village councils was of ancient origin. An experienced British officer described the system as follows: "The village council was composed of the head of every family residing within its limits, however low his rank, or small his property: from this tribunal, there was an appeal to the district council, which consisted of intelligent delegates from each village." Ward revived these councils and gave them the necessary authority to maintain existing irrigation works. In addition important disused works were repaired under the supervision of government engineers, mainly at government expense.

In 1860 Ward was succeeded by Sir Charles Justin Mac-Carthy. The new governor had followed Sir Emerson Tennent as Colonial Secretary in 1851 and was thus familiar with Ceylon's problems. The fiasco over the Colombo–Kandy railway had created the impression in London that the Ceylon Government was not to be trusted where financial matters were concerned. MacCarthy was compelled to enforce rigid economy— "niggardly cheeseparing" as one of his subordinates called it. Once again the roads fell into disrepair and no new construction was undertaken.

This led, as was to be expected, to a good deal of criticism from the European community. The Europeans argued that it was unfair to expect the island to contribute to its own defence as the garrison was maintained largely for imperial purposes. It would be possible to spend £100,000 on improving the roads, if the full cost of defence were met by the Imperial Government. The London Government maintained that the cost of colonial garrisons should normally be met by the resources of the colony, and that Ceylon was no exception.

MacCarthy seems to have added to the discontent by his rigid policy of economy. In three years he accumulated a surplus of more than £500,000. The opposition of the people increased, and in 1864 the unofficial members of the Legislative Council took advantage of the absence of a number of officials to censure the government by a snap vote. This vote had no effect on official policy as the governor could over-

I

ride decisions of the Legislative Council. After several weeks of tension, the unofficial members resigned in protest. The governor consulted his Executive Council and decided to reject the resignations.

The events of 1864 caused great indignation among the Europeans and politically-conscious Ceylonese. For once there was no question of a clash of interests between the Europeans and the natives of Ceylon, and a political organization called the Ceylon League was created. The main aim of the Ceylon League was to secure an unofficial majority on the Legislative Council, an aim which was not realized until more than half a century had elapsed. The Colonial Office was adamant in refusing all concessions. The idealism of Colebrooke had given way to an unimaginative and sterile policy of caution.

The deadlock was ended, not by a generous gesture from the government, nor by an abandonment by the unofficial members of their declared aims, but by an era of economic prosperity which enabled Sir Hercules Robinson, MacCarthy's successor as governor, to embark on a more vigorous policy in regard to roads. Robinson was one of the ablest British colonial administrators of the century—modest, diligent, sensible, "the most painstaking, hardworking man I have ever met," as a colleague described him. He took a keen interest in the system of village councils which had been revived by Ward and given responsibility for irrigation. In 1871 these councils were given greatly extended powers and responsibilities for local affairs. In addition municipal councils with elected majorities were set up in Colombo and two other large towns. These were extremely important advances because the educated classes, and especially the politically minded, were given an outlet for their energies. They gained practical experience of public administration, and the way was thus paved for the introduction of popular democracy.

The success of these experiments in local democracy depended, of course, on the existence of an educated and alert citizenry. During Robinson's period as governor the number of government schools increased sharply and by 1872 there were 200 government schools with 10,000 pupils: at the same time there were 400 Christian mission schools with 25,000 pupils as well as schools sponsored by Buddhists, Hindus and Moslems. It was at this time that the coffee industry reached the peak of its prosperity. Exports had risen from 178,603 cwt. in 1845 to over a million cwt. in 1870. Large numbers of Indian immigrants arrived each year to work as plantation labourers. In 1868, however, almost unnoticed, there appeared a blight popularly known as the Coffee Bug. Production began to decline and exports decreased. "The leaf disease got worse and worse, and men got madder and madder, and prices got higher and higher, and crops got smaller and smaller." Exports were destined to decline to such an extent that by 1886 they were down to the 1845 level, three years later to the 1840 level. By the turn of the century coffee was no longer of any importance in the commercial life of Ceylon.

Robinson was succeeded as governor by Sir William Henry Gregory, another man of great charm and ability. Gregory had served for some years in the House of Commons where he had won the respect of political friends and enemies alike. He was a man of independent views. On his first day in Ceylon he decided that the house maintained at Galle for entertaining illustrious visitors "was entirely unnecessary, except to afford to the Downing Street officials the means of exercising hospitality at the expense of Ceylon". He decided to sell the building, but knowing that the Colonial Office would refuse their sanction, Gregory acted first and informed the Secretary of State afterwards. He received "an angry despatch" and replied with what he called a "penitent, but somewhat sarcastic missive".

Gregory was soon immersed in the Coffee Bug crisis. The magnitude of the trouble was at first masked by the high prices which coffee was fetching, and it was difficult for the government to convince the planters that coffee production might never return to its previous high levels. Gregory was fortunate in having the skilled advice of Dr. G. H. K. Thwaites, who from 1849 to 1880 was superintendent of the Royal Botanic Gardens at Kandy. Thwaites was described by an acquaintance as "a strange, morose old gentleman, who seemed to prefer the life of a hermit to that of the average man . . . brief in his words, and cold in his manner". "I learned much from him,

as he was a man of general information and of deep research,"
wrote Gregory. "I much wish I had attended to his wise
admonitions as to the instability of coffee. Year after year he
foretold its downfall, year after year he was subjected to obloquy
and ridicule for his disloyalty to the great King Coffee."
Thwaites realized that salvation lay in a diversification of
agriculture and had experimented with cinchona (quinine) and
a number of varieties of tea.

Emerson Tennent, writing in 1859, mentioned as an evident
curiosity some tea plants which had been grown as an experiment. The cultivation of tea had been attempted by the Dutch,
he wrote, but without success. Gradually Thwaites was able to
persuade the planters to grow small quantities of tea. In 1873
some 250 acres were planted with tea: ten years later the acreage
was 35,000: in ten more years the acreage under tea had risen
to 275,000: in the next fifty years the acreage had again doubled.
Today tea is Ceylon's most important crop, accounting for
more than half the total value of the exports of the island.

The rate at which the new tea industry expanded was
rapid, perhaps too rapid. A planter of experience wrote as
follows:

"One of the worst aspects of the fierce burst of energy
and courage with which the coffee planters faced the ruin
of their old industry was the speed with which they opened
up the new tea lands. With an almost savage disregard for
the greatest principle in agriculture—that more must be put
into land than is taken from it—they felled huge areas of
virgin forests covering the hills, without protective measures
of soil conservation, so that the accumulated treasure of
milleniums, agriculturally speaking—the wonderful rich top
and subsoil of thousands of years of forest growth and protection—were swept away in the first rains. The heritage of
a millenium could, and did, rush down the hillsides in a
single monsoon season, a reckless dissipation of natural resources for which the industry has paid heavily ever since.
It was some time before the ruinous folly of these proceedings was realized and steps taken to see that it did not
happen again. . . ."

Thwaites was also interested in growing cinchona, and as in the case of tea he was able to stimulate the planters to grow it in increasing quantities. The acreage under cinchona increased from 500 in 1872 to more than 100 times as much ten years later. Exports realized about £1,300 in 1876, about £365,000 in 1883. But as production increased, the price declined, and planters who had been getting over 12s. an ounce in 1878 found they could only get 2s. an ounce ten years later. In time the planting of cinchona virtually ceased. It was, however, revived during the Second World War when 125 acres were planted to supply local needs in the event of the cessation of foreign supplies.

Another feature of Governor Gregory's conduct of affairs was his policy of entrusting the native chiefs with a good deal of responsibility for administration. At times in the past, and especially after the disturbances of 1817-8 and 1848, there had been a reaction away from this policy: there had been a natural disposition to regard the native chiefs as potential rebels. One official contended "that the Kandian chiefs acted tyrannically, that conceding power to them was giving them illegitimate influence, and that it was unjust to the lowly born Kandian that he should be prejudiced by reason of birth". But memories of past disturbances were fading, and, moreover, a number of governors had experienced more trouble from the European and Burgher communities than from the natives. Gregory held the view that the Kandyan provinces should, as far as possible, "be ruled by means of the old Kandian families, that is, by appointing efficient men, when they could be obtained, representatives of these families. The Kandian population is intensely aristocratic, and the influence of the chiefs very great. . . . Matters went on far more smoothly and efficiently when the native officers were selected from families of ancient lineage rather than from men who, though of excellent character and of experience, had risen from the ranks".

There was, of course, some opposition to Gregory's policy in this respect both from British officials and the new educated classes in Ceylon. These people argued that the old system of chiefs was doomed and would have to be replaced by modern ideas of parliamentary government and local democracy; to revive the old system of hereditary native chiefs was to perpetuate an anachronism.

Considerable reforms stand to Gregory's credit. He devoted substantial sums to prison reform and to extending the work of the medical department. The mass of the people, wrote Gregory, "were still at the mercy of ignorant quacks and devil-dancers. This state of things reflected discredit on our government". As a first step to improve the situation he established a chain of small dispensaries in rural areas. The provincial boundaries were revised, increasing the number of provinces from six to nine.

Another great event which occurred during Gregory's administration, and one for which Gregory himself must take a good deal of credit, was the construction of the harbour at Colombo. The completion of the Suez Canal in 1869 had increased the importance of Ceylon which now lay on the direct route from Europe to the Far East and Australasia. What was needed in Ceylon was a good harbour which could be of service to the increasing numbers of merchant vessels: Galle harbour would have to be improved, or a new harbour constructed at Colombo. Either course would involve heavy expenditure. The Colonial Office in London favoured the plan to improve Galle. The Under-Secretary told Gregory not to bother with "the wild scheme" of constructing a new harbour at Colombo. It was typical of Gregory that, though he had originally favoured Galle, he took up the Colombo plan with enthusiasm when he was convinced by the experts of its advantages. Work began on the new harbour in 1873.

CHAPTER X

CONSOLIDATION, 1877-1918

Better to plough deep than wide.—Tamil proverb.

CEYLON had been lucky in the five governors who served in the thirty critical years after the Kandyan disturbances of 1848. Gregory was a man of outstanding ability. Robinson and Ward were hardly less competent, and Anderson was probably above the average of British Colonial Governors of the period. If MacCarthy's administration was less forceful and imaginative, it must be remembered that the Treasury in London was making it impossible for the Ceylon Government to embark on ambitious schemes of public works, however necessary these may have seemed in Ceylon.

The period of forty years covered by this chapter was a time of steady consolidation rather than spectacular development. There were no outstanding peaks of achievement. The record, rather, is concerned with solid advance, with such prosaic but important things as sanitation and postal services. What was required from the governors and officials was not so much outstanding brilliance as diligence, integrity, and a sympathy for the aspirations of the Ceylonese. The eight men who served as governor between 1877 and 1918 possessed these qualities. Sir Arthur Hamilton-Gordon (afterwards Lord Stanmore) and his successor Sir Arthur Havelock were both extremely competent administrators and popular with the people. Only one governor, Sir Robert (afterwards Lord) Chambers can be regarded as having been a square peg in a round hole.

Sir William Gregory was succeeded as governor by Sir James Longden. The fall in revenue, caused by the spread of the Coffee Bug and the consequent depression, curtailed expenditure on public works. When Hamilton-Gordon took over in 1883 things had begun to improve. Exports of cinchona had been increasing and the price had only just begun to fall. Cultivation of tea on a commercial scale was beginning.

Hamilton-Gordon was a man of wide experience. He had served in the House of Commons as a Liberal from 1854-7 and had acted as private secretary to Gladstone for a time. He spent a considerable sum of money on irrigation works, roads, railways and telegraph lines. He introduced a new penal code and a criminal procedure code. He also took some interest in the educational system. The Christian missionaries had for long concerned themselves intimately with education. "They are all working away at high pressure," Gregory had written, "and if they do not convert, they certainly civilize." The standard of education of the people was, however, low if measured in terms of literacy. In Hamilton-Gordon's time the proportion of those who could read or write was only one in four for men, only one in twenty-five for women. Educational work was not confined to the government and the Christian missions. Both Buddhist and Hindu educational institutions were established. There was, indeed, a revival of interest in these religions, stimulated in part by the proselytizing activities of the Christian missionaries, in part by the work of the Theosophical Society, one of whose leaders visited Ceylon and embraced the Buddhist faith.

In the last year of Hamilton-Gordon's period of office a small change was made in the composition of the Legislative Council. The change was overdue. "The governor," wrote a foreign visitor to Ceylon at this time, "is pretty nearly an unlimited monarch, and troubles himself but little with the decisions of his parliament of councillors. Most of the defects in the administration of affairs under which this fine island suffers are attributed to this absolute power of an individual, and it is certainly not at all to the taste of the consitutional English." The Legislative Council had been created after the publication of the Colebrooke report more than half a century earlier. It had originally consisted of the governor, nine officials, and a number of unofficial members nominated by the governor. It had for some time been urged by the unofficial members, and admitted by the officials, that Ceylonese representation ought to be increased. The suggestion that the unofficial members should be elected was, however, unacceptable to the government, as was the claim for an unofficial majority. A small concession towards increasing the representative character of the Council was, however, made in 1889 when two more nominated unofficial members were added, one being a Kandyan Sinhalese and one a Moslem. This minor reform left the powers of the council unaltered and continued the official majority.

Sir Joseph West Ridgeway succeeded to the governorship in 1896. Ridgeway, wrote an acquaintance, was "brilliant and far-sighted . . . one of the wisest, and most able of our rulers . . . a very shrewd and sympathetic statesman possessed of the heaven-born gift of being able to select the right man for the right place at the right time". He was keenly interested in agriculture and created a special irrigation department and a veterinary department. Coffee and cinchona continued to decline in importance, but there was a slight improvement in the cultivation and export of cinnamon, cocoa, and tobacco, and a great expansion in the production of tea, rubber, and coco-nut products. The acreage under tea increased, though the rate of increase began to slacken off after 1900 and even declined slightly towards the end of Ridgeway's administration. Methods of cultivation improved, however, and exports rose from 110 million lb. in 1896 to 170 million lb. ten years later.

The cultivation of rubber also expanded greatly as new methods of cultivation were discovered. Rubber had been introduced as early as 1876, the first plants being obtained from the Royal Botanical Gardens at Kew. Cultivation was not remunerative at first, but with the expansion of the automobile industry the demand for rubber increased and the price jumped spectacularly, trebling in the space of a few years. Less than a thousand acres were under rubber when Ridgeway arrived in Ceylon: when he left in 1903 the figure had increased to over 11,000 acres. Rubber production has always been speculative because of its fluctuating price on the world market.

The products of the coco-nut palm formed the third staple export. The important role that the coco-nut palm was destined to play in the economic life of Ceylon had been foreseen in the early years of the century by a remarkable official, Anthony

Bertolacci, who had served under North. In a book published in 1817 he wrote:

"Above all things, the promoting of a large export of coco-nut oil to the English markets is to be recommended. More may be done for Ceylon by that means, than by almost any other that can be devised. By the opening of a great market for that commodity, Ceylon may be made rich beyond our present expectations."

The value of exports of coco-nuts, coco-nut oil, copra (dried coco-nut kernels), dessicated coco-nuts, coco-nut fibre, and other coco-nut products doubled while Ridgeway was governor.

Prosperity in the plantations attracted a growing number of immigrant labourers from India. The Ceylon Government facilitated the process of immigration by tax concessions to plantation labourers. Steps were taken to improve the medical conditions in the estates and to prevent the introduction of cholera, small-pox, and other diseases.

Ridgeway was also concerned with the conditions of the peasantry. Irrigation was further improved, educational facilities increased, and medical services extended. The better morale and discipline in the public service was a reflection of the new prosperity.

Sir Henry Blake followed Ridgeway as governor, serving in Ceylon from 1903 to 1907. Cultivation of rubber continued to increase rapidly, the cultivated acreage growing from 11,000 in 1903 to 150,000 in 1907. The price was high and big profits were made. Tea exports increased slightly after the setback about 1900 when prices had been low. Coco-nut exports also increased during this period.

Sir Henry McCallum succeeded Blake in 1907. McCallum instituted a number of reforms in the Civil Service, approved a revision of the criminal code, extended irrigation works, and expanded the school system. He was, however, largely occupied with the rising demand for political reform.

The growth of a prosperous educated middle class of Ceylonese, due in part to the general prosperity of the island and in part to the steadily improving educational facilities, began to have an effect on political affairs. An increasing number of Ceylonese were entering the professions, and they were naturally not content with the subordinate position they occupied in political life. Most of the senior government posts were held by British officials, and those Ceylonese who had administrative responsibilities in the interior were nearly all descendants of the old nobility. There were differences of opinion about the wisdom of perpetuating the hereditary system by giving power to the old aristocracy. Sir William Gregory believed there was no alternative and encouraged it. Sir Henry McCallum took the same view and even revived the durbar (levee) of chiefs.

The Executive Council retained the entirely official character which it had been given in 1833. The Legislative Council had an official majority, and the unofficial members were all selected by the governor. Successive governors did what they could, in nominating unofficial members, to choose persons who were representative of the best elements in Ceylonese life, but the temptation to choose 'reliable' people was sometimes too strong to be resisted.

A number of external factors inspired the Ceylonese to demand political rights. The principle of election to legislative bodies had been introduced in India in the last decade of the nineteenth century. There was a further extension of the elective principle in India in 1909, and for the first time the Viceroy's Executive Council included an Indian. The defeat of Russia by Japan in 1904-5 had given a tremendous fillip to the nationalist movements of Asia.

The leading Ceylonese now demanded the abolition of the system of communal representation on the Legislative Council and of the principle of gubernatorial nomination. Instead they wanted to have the unofficial members elected for territorial constituencies, even if on a limited franchise. They were willing to see the minority communities—such as the Europeans, Burghers, and Moslems—represented by nominees of the governor if these communities were otherwise unrepresented. They also asked for some unofficial representation on the Executive Council.

The concessions made by the British Government to these demands were niggardly. The constitution of the Executive

Council remained unaltered. The unofficial representation on the Legislative Council was increased from eight to ten, but as this would have given the unofficial members a majority of one, the official representation was simultaneously increased to eleven. Of the ten unofficial members, six were nominated by the governor as before but four were now elected on a communal basis—two representing the Europeans, one the Burgher community, and one the Educated Ceylonese— "a purely imaginary community", was how a British official described them, ". . . one of the curiosities of political history."

It was unfortunate that discontent with the small extent of these reforms should coincide with the appointment of Sir Robert (afterwards Lord) Chalmers. Chalmers was a man of great ability—he could speak Pali—but he was unhappy in Ceylon. He was misjudged by the Ceylonese, who disliked his personal idiosyncrasies and ignored his undoubted administrative gifts. He later became Master of Peterhouse, Cambridge.

In 1915 political discontent found expression in a number of riots, in some cases being religious in origin. The fact that Britain was at war seems to have unnerved the Ceylon Government. Chalmers certainly exaggerated the gravity of the situation and suppressed the disturbances with unnecessary severity. Martial law was declared and a number of undoubtedly innocent persons were executed. Many of the people who were later to obtain positions of leadership and distinction in political life— including Mr. Senanayake, the present Prime Minister—came to the fore during this period. It is a remarkable tribute to their good sense that so few of them became embittered by their experiences during the 1915 riots and subsequently.

An indirect result of the disturbances was the organization of political parties and associations to demand political reforms. In 1917 the Ceylon Reform League was created and joined with the Ceylon National Association in demanding that the Legislative Council should have a majority of unofficial members who should be elected for territorial constituencies. This demand was again rejected.

The years of the First World War saw the genesis of the nationalist movement in Ceylon. Nationalism is a complex political idea, compounded of many elements. It was one of the main forces in European politics during the nineteenth century, and in 1868, with the Meiji Restoration, the idea took root in Japan; not long afterwards it had spread to China and India.

Nationalism in Asia was sometimes revolutionary in form—as it was in China—sometimes constitutional and reformist—as it was in Ceylon and for many years in India. Nationalism can become exaggerated and extreme in the hands of unscrupulous demagogues, but in Ceylon it was usually reasonable and moderate. The heterogeneous nature of the population made it impossible to adopt the extravagant racial, religious, and linguistic theories which elsewhere were used to stimulate a feeling of national solidarity. There were no 'pure' races in Ceylon: four different religions were accepted by substantial sections of the population: different languages and dialects were spoken, and English, the only language which had no communal connotation for the nationalists, had been imported from another continent: the monarchical system, so often a stimulus to nationalism, had ended ignominiously a century earlier.

Ceylon, being geographically close to India and inhabited by people in many ways akin to the peoples of India, was influenced by the development of the nationalist movement on the mainland. In 1917 the Secretary of State for India had made an important pronouncement which, though not formally extended to Ceylon or other British colonies, was widely assumed to be a definition of the general aims of British colonial policy.

"The policy of His Majesty's Government . . . is that of the increasing association of Indians in every branch of the administration and the gradual development of self-governing institutions with a view to the progressive realization of responsible government in India as an integral part of the British Empire."

The importance of this statement for Ceylonese nationalists was that it envisaged the attainment by non-British peoples of the same constitutional status as had been achieved by the people of British stock in the older dominions. There were, of course, those who disliked the absence of a time-table, who mistrusted phrases like "gradual development" and "progressive realization". And the insistence on India's remaining an integral part of the British Empire was regarded as a limitation of freedom, though it was presently agreed that once a country had become independent it could, in fact, secede from the Empire—as was to happen in the case of Ireland and Burma.

That the Ceylon Government should resist a too rapid realization of self-government was perhaps natural, though caution was often carried to excess. During the first half of the nineteenth century, the public service in Ceylon had consisted of persons who, though paternalistic, had often been slack and inefficient. After the 1848 disturbances a determined effort had been made to improve discipline and morale. By the end of the century Ceylon possessed an administration of great efficiency, and there was no breath of corruption among the senior officials. To open the public service and institutions of government to the Ceylonese without restriction would inevitably lead to a difficult period of adjustment in which the previous high standards might have to be abandoned temporarily.

The Ceylonese leaders admitted that there might be initial difficulties, but as it was manifestly impossible to keep the native people in a subordinate position indefinitely, the sooner reforms were introduced, the better for both Ceylon and Britain. Thus there began a period of struggle which was to last a generation.

CHAPTER XI

THE STRUGGLE FOR INDEPENDENCE, 1918-48

"There ought to be nothing to preclude the hope, when the growth of a colonial possession is such as to make separation from the mother country a natural and beneficial result, that that separation, so far from being effected by violence and bloodshed, might be in the result of a peaceable and friendly transaction. Surely it is a great object to place, if possible, our colonial policy on such a footing, not for the purpose of bringing about a separation, but of providing a guarantee that, if separation should occur, it should be in a friendly way."—William Ewart Gladstone, in the House of Commons, 26th April, 1870.

THIS chapter is concerned only with political matters. During the three decades following the First World War many changes —economic, social, cultural—were, of course, taking place in Ceylon. But in the minds of the majority of educated Ceylonese the political struggle predominated. A brief survey of the non-political developments during this period will be included in the final chapter.

The thirty years covered by this chapter fall into three distinct periods. From 1918 until 1931 the structure of government in Ceylon followed the general lines of the recommendations which Colebrooke had put forward in 1832. There was a governor, an executive council on which officials were in a majority, and a legislative council on which, after 1920, the unofficial members were in a majority. From 1931 to 1946 there was a novel form of government in which both executive and legislative functions were vested in an elected State Council. In 1946 the orthodox cabinet system of government, with a bi-cameral legislature, was introduced.

*　　*　　*　　*　　*

In 1919 the Ceylon National Congress was formed, consisting of leaders of opinion in all the main communities. The chief inspiration, however, came from the Low Country Sinhalese; and after a few years most of the Tamils broke away and formed a separate organization. The National Congress put forward precise demands for constitutional reform. They asked for a greatly enlarged legislative council, four-fifths of the members of which should be elected for territorial constituencies, and for unofficial representation on the Executive Council. This latter demand was granted in 1920 and the Executive Council, which for ninety years had consisted of five senior officials, was widened to include three unofficial members. At the same time the Legislative Council was increased to a membership of thirty-seven: fourteen of the members were officials, and of the unofficial members eleven were elected for territorial constituencies.

This was a real advance, but agitation for further progress began at once. Now that there was a substantial unofficial element in the Legislature, demands for political reform could be expressed through constitutional channels, and in 1921 a resolution sponsored by the President of the National Congress was debated in the Legislative Council.

The main points in the resolution were:

(i) That the Legislative Council should again be increased in size, and that the majority of the members should be elected on a territorial basis.

(ii) That the council should no longer be presided over by the governor but by a Speaker elected by itself.

(iii) That three of the territorially-elected members of the Legislative Council should serve on the Executive Council as ministers in charge of departments of government.

The main aims of these proposals were to increase the representative character of the Government and to reduce the extent of, but not abolish, communal representation. The National Congress, "while totally opposed on principle to communal representation as inimical to the political progress of the country, has agreed that the special representation of the minorities should continue". The governor, Sir William Manning, was opposed to the abandonment of communal representation: he told the Secretary of State that to do so would mean that the Sinhalese "could obtain an overwhelming proportion of electoral power and reduce all other communities, severally and collectively, to political impotence". The Secretary of State shared this view: he thought that communal representation would have to continue "for an indefinite period".

Discussions on further reform continued for two years, and in December 1923 the Secretary of State sanctioned certain changes which went part of the way to meeting the demands of the National Congress. The official representation on the Legislative Council was reduced from fourteen to twelve and the unofficial representation increased to thirty-seven, of whom twenty-three were elected for territorial constituencies. The request for the right to elect a Speaker was met by the election of a vice-president of the council who would ordinarily preside. The powers of the council were changed slightly but were still limited, as the governor could declare any matter before it to be of paramount importance to the public interest, in which case only the official members could vote. The composition of the Executive Council remained unaltered.

The system of government before 1931 was described as follows by a distinguished Ceylon official:

"Under the Crown Colony system, the Governor for the time being is personally and directly responsible to the Secretary of State for the Colonies for the good government of the territory under his administration; and, though he is assisted by an Executive Council, is under statutory obligation to act with its concurrence in a large number of instances, and is required to report to the Secretary of State any case in which he has decided to reject the advice tendered to him by a majority of its members, he, as His Majesty's Representative in the Colony, is the Chief Executive, all orders being issued and all public acts done by him or in his name. . . ."

*   *   *   *   *

This was the constitution which was described as "an unqualified failure" by the members of the Donoughmore Com-

K

mission who visited Ceylon in 1927 -8. To the commissioners the most striking feature of the constitution was the divorce of power from responsibility. The unofficial members formed the overwhelming majority of the Legislative Council, yet they had no responsibility for the conduct of public business: the official members, on the other hand, had such a responsibility but were in a permanent minority. "Thus, on a counting of heads, those who have the controlling votes in the council are not called upon to bear the responsibility for their decisions: those who have to bear the responsibility are without the controlling votes." The inevitable consequence was a breach between the nominated official and the elected unofficial members. "Denied all prospects of office, the unofficial members were in no danger of being called upon to translate their criticisms into action and to execute in practice the measures which they advocated." The conciliatory policy which the Government pursued did not lead the unofficial members to abandon their position as hostile critics. The absence of any party system was, in the view of the commission, "a serious handicap to the development of responsible parliamentary institutions".

Particularly acute difficulties were encountered in the Council's Finance Committee, which consisted of the unofficial members under the chairmanship of the Colonial Secretary, together with the Controller of Revenue and the Colonial Treasurer. "It has become the practice for Heads of Departments to be treated as hostile witnesses. . . . Questions are rarely confined to the matters at issue. . . . Under a constant fire of uninstructed criticism, subjected to grave discourtesy, if not on occasion to personal insult, and denied the protection that is their due, it is not surprising that these officers find the treatment extended to them painful and humiliating."

Blame for this development could not fairly be laid at the door of the Ceylonese politicians who had been elected to the Legislative Council. They were, like the British officials, the victims of a system which had not evolved rapidly enough to keep pace with the aspirations and capabilities of a nation.

Some people felt that the Donoughmore Commissioners had painted an unduly gloomy picture of the working of the constitution. Sir Herbert Stanley, the governor from 1927 to 1931, wrote in a letter to the Secretary of State for the Colonies that he could not accept the view of the commissioners that the Constitution was an unqualified failure. "The operation of the present Constitution has proved a qualified success rather than an unqualified failure. . . . The picture presented in the report is a little overdrawn." He thought the description of the operation of the Finance Committee was misleading. There might have been occasions when "the heat of argument has induced an over-emphasis of diction", but such occurrences had been comparatively rare.

The Special Commission, whose comments are quoted above, had been appointed in August 1927 to investigate the working of the Constitution and consider proposals for revision. It was a strong commission, consisting of the Earl of Donoughmore (chairman), Sir Matthew Nathan, Sir Geoffrey Butler, and Dr. (later Sir) Drummond Shiels.

The commissioners were anxious "not slavishly to follow the forms and practice of the British model". They recommended the creation of a State Council in place of the Legislative Council. This State Council would have sixty-five members elected territorially, three *ex officio* members, without a vote, known as Officers of State, and up to twelve persons nominated by the governor to increase the Council's representative character. Both executive and legislative functions would be vested in this Council.

The Council would be divided into seven committees, the subjects entrusted to them being home affairs, agriculture, local administration, health, education, public works, and communications. Each committee would elect a chairman who would then be in effect a minister in control of a department of government. The seven ministers, together with the three *ex officio* members, would then form a Board of Ministers, or cabinet, the *ex officio* members taking part in the discussions but not voting. The chief secretary would be chairman of the board, and the board itself would elect a vice-chairman, who would be *ex officio* the Leader of the State Council. The Council would elect its own Speaker. The governor would have supervisory rather than executive powers, "but his executive powers being diminished his reserve powers would be proportionately increased". He would, in fact, have "the unqualified right to refuse or reserve his assent".

The commission recommended two main changes in the electoral system. They found that only 4 per cent of the population was entitled to vote, and they recommended that the suffrage be extended to all men over twenty-one and all women over thirty who applied to be registered as electors and had resided in the island for at least five years. Income, property and literacy qualifications would be abolished. The consequence of the introduction of adult suffrage would be to increase the electorate from about 205,000 to 1,850,000, almost a tenfold increase.

As regards communal representation, the commissioners commented as follows:

"Communal representation was devised with a view to assisting the development of democratic institutions in countries of different races and religions and in the hope of eliminating the clash of these various interests during elections. It was expected to provide, peacefully, an effective legislative assembly which would give a fair representation of the different elements in the population and would also tend to promote unity. Unfortunately, the experiment has not given the desired results, but has had, if anything, the opposite effect. The representatives of the various communities do not trust one another, and communal representation has not helped to develop a uniting bond or link. . . .

We have come unhesitatingly to the conclusion that communal representation is, as it were, a canker on the body politic, eating deeper and deeper into the vital energies of the people, breeding self-interest, suspicion and animosity, poisoning the new growth of political consciousness, and effectively preventing the development of a national or corporate spirit. . . . There can be no hope of binding together the diverse elements of the population in a realization of their common kinship and an acknowledgment of common obligations to the country of which they are all citizens as long as the system of communal representation, with all its disintegrating influences, remains a distinctive feature of the constitution."

Accordingly they recommended the abolition of the system. With regard to the Kandyan problem, the origin of which has been referred to in earlier chapters, they recommended no special treatment for the Kandyan provinces beyond a suggestion that the State Council might occasionally meet at Kandy. "It is our confident hope that their pride in their ancient Kingdom and historic institutions will form part of a national protagonism and that the Kandyan identity will best be preserved, and receive its noblest fulfilment, in the growth and final emergence of a strong and united Ceylonese nation."

The commissioners also recommended certain changes in the system of local administration and in the civil and public services.

The recommendations of the Donoughmore Commission were both bold and imaginative, and it is difficult to recall the amazement with which they were greeted. A distinguished official in London described the report as "a disconcerting phenomenon . . . its proposals are such as to take away the breath of the experienced official . . . a surprising document . . . ingenious and original . . . this adventurous report . . . a work of insight and genius". Sir Herbert Stanley, the governor, recognized that the proposed system would not be an easy one to work, and said so in a letter to the Secretary of State. If in the end it proved a failure, he intimated, this would not necessarily imply that the people of Ceylon were unfitted for self-government.

The report was published in July 1928, and a series of debates on the main recommendations were initiated in the Legislative Council.

It is usually the case in the development of self-government that each new instalment of constitutional advance, however great, is immediately attacked as being inadequate. It is believed, and probably with some measure of truth, that if there is a complacent acceptance of what is newly given, there is no likelihood of any advance in the near future. A good deal of criticism to which the Donoughmore Constitution was subjected may be discounted on these grounds.

The system of executive committees which the commissioners had proposed came in for particular criticism in the Legislative Council, and the unofficial members voted by twenty-three votes to eight that it was "not suited to local conditions" and "unacceptable to the people". The unofficial members also opposed the proposal that the ministers should be elected by the executive committees, preferring that they should be elected by the whole Council. There was also opposition to the proposed extensions of the governor's powers and to certain features of the proposed franchise provisions.

There were, of course, valid arguments both for and against the proposals of the Donoughmore Commission and the amendments to them demanded by the Legislative Council. But the Donoughmore Commissioners had sought to devise a balanced arrangement, and the consequence of considering each item in the proposed new constitution in isolation and amending it was to produce an entirely new constitutional scheme. Eventually, the Secretary of State, Lord Passfield (Sidney Webb), authorized the governor to say that "while no doubt modifications in detail will be necessary", the recommendations "must be regarded as a whole".

In October 1929 Lord Passfield announced that the commission's main recommendations would be put into operation, and the unofficial members of the Legislative Council voted by a narrow majority in favour of this course. The main modifications in the Donoughmore scheme made by the Secretary of State were to reduce the size of the State Council from eighty to sixty-one members, to give women the vote at twenty-one rather than thirty, and to require persons not domiciled in Ceylon (mainly Indians) to produce a certificate of 'permanent residence' before they could be enrolled as voters.

*　　*　　*　　*　　*

Looking back on the Donoughmore Constitution in the light of its operation, it is not difficult to discern its main strengths and weaknesses. The commissioners intended that it should be of a transitional character, paving the way for eventual self-government. The sweeping extension of the franchise was a courageous and revolutionary reform. For the first time an Asian country had universal suffrage without literacy, property, income, or sex qualifications. The abandonment of communal representation, though condemned at the time by some minority groups, had the long-term effect—as was intended by the commissioners—of decreasing communal hostility and creating a spirit of national solidarity and unity. The combination of executive and legislative functions in one organ of government, though novel, did avoid the weakness of the earlier constitution in which power and responsibility were divorced.

The constitution gave responsibility to Ceylonese ministers for the first time. It is true the responsibility was limited, but it included the subject of finance for which the Board of Ministers was collectively responsible. The committee system, however, made impossible the development of collective ministerial responsibility except when the Board of Ministers met as a finance committee. Each minister was bound by the votes of his own committee and might find himself in the difficult position of having to defend in the Board of Ministers or the State Council a policy favoured by his committee but with which he himself disagreed. The Donoughmore Commission had foreseen this possibility but did not regard it as likely to be frequent or serious.

One advantage of the committee system should be mentioned. If a minister showed himself to be incompetent, it was possible for him to be dismissed and replaced, without other ministers being directly affected. Under the normal cabinet system, a vote of no-confidence in an individual minister entails the resignation of the whole ministry.

The position of the three Officers of State evoked some criticism. The commissioners had intended that they should act as advisers and counsellors. They were not entitled to vote, and the commissioners took the view that this part of the new constitution could be abandoned in time without upsetting the rest of the system. In the event, largely because of the illness of the governor, the duties of the Officers of State became magnified, and many Ceylonese came to the conclusion that the Officers of State wielded the same powers as they had before the introduction of the Donoughmore Constitution.

One aspect of the working of the Donoughmore Constitution which was criticized was the intense concentration of discussion in the State Council on matters of administrative detail rather than broad policy. This was particularly so with regard to the personnel of the public service. "The idea of influence in high quarters," wrote Sir Andrew Caldecott, Governor of Ceylon from 1937 to 1944, "dies hard in England. . . . In the East the idea has not yet begun to die; men in a position to do so are expected by relatives and friends to promote their advancement as a matter of course. There is indeed nothing intrinsically immoral about nepotism; but it is directly contrary to our accepted principles of equalization of opportunity and appointment by worth. It was in my opinion unfair to the executive committees ever to have placed their members in a position in which conflicts of loyalties were bound to arise".

This concentration in the State Council on matters of administrative detail was not, of course, a defect of the Donoughmore Constitution as such. If there were a desire to discuss detailed questions of departmental administration rather than general policy, no constitutional arrangement could suppress it. Indeed, the Donoughmore Commissioners claimed to have had this difficulty very much in mind in devising the new constitution. Accepting the fact that the politicians and people of Ceylon were greatly interested in administrative details, the commissioners deliberately created a system in which such matters could be openly discussed.

It has been said that the committee system militated against the organization of political parties with coherent policies, a defect which the Donoughmore Commissioners had noted in the earlier constitution. There is, of course, no reason in theory why political parties should not flourish in any democratic form of government. The abolition of communal representation was intended to eliminate artificial barriers and facilitate the evolution of genuine and coherent parties. The fact that ideological parties, as opposed to communal parties, were slow in growing could not be ascribed solely to the committee system, although there is no doubt that the Donoughmore Constitution proved disappointing in this respect. The evolution of parties "is indeed improbable, if not impossible, under the present system [the Donoughmore Constitution] which affords no opportunity for the fall and rise in ministries, for the moulding and crystallization of policies, and thereby for orientated government and orientated opposition. Until this evolution takes place and there are before the electorate political programmes on which a vote can be intelligently given for this side or for that, electioneering must tend to consist in a parade of personalities, irresponsible promises, and objectionable appeals to race, caste or creed." So wrote Caldecott to the Secretary of State.

*   *   *   *   *

Elections for the new State Council were held in 1931, and members were returned as follows:

Sinhalese: Low Country	..	28
,, Kandyan ..	..	10
Ceylon Tamils	..	3
Indian Tamils	..	2
Europeans	..	2
Moslems	..	1
Unfilled	..	4

Many of the Ceylon Tamils boycotted the election either as a protest against the abolition of communal representation or because they believed that the new constitution did not provide sufficient self-government, so four seats which would probably have gone to them were unfilled. On a strictly communal population basis, the Low Country Sinhalese and the Europeans were over-represented, and all other communities under-represented. The governor filled the seats reserved for his nominees with four Europeans, two Burghers, one Indian Tamil, and one Moslem.

No sooner had the new State Council come into existence than demands for its reform were voiced. There were different views on the precise changes that were considered desirable, but the majority view—which was of necessity substantially Sinhalese—was that three main changes were necessary.

(i) The replacement of the three Officers of State by elected members of the State Council, a change which the Donough-more Commissioners had themselves considered desirable as soon as possible.

(ii) The election of a chief minister by the whole State Council: the chief minister would then function as a prime minister and allot portfolios to his colleagues in the State Council, and the ministry would be collectively responsible to the State Council.

(iii) The curtailment of the governor's special powers.

On points (i) and (iii) there was almost unanimity among the Ceylonese, but there was disagreement on point (ii) between the Sinhalese and the minority communities. The minorities feared that the adoption of the second proposal would facilitate the creation of a ministry from which the minorities were excluded, whereas under the Donoughmore Constitution they believed they could always hope to hold some ministerial posts, and in fact held two of the seven posts at that time.

Between the middle of 1932 and the middle of 1934 there were frequent debates in the State Council, consultations between the ministers and the governor, and communications between Ceylon and the Secretary of State, Sir Philip Cunliffe-Lister (later Viscount Swinton). Although it was generally recognized that the Donoughmore Constitution required further development (a view which the governor shared) the Secretary of State believed that it ought to remain in operation for the time being. His decision was influenced in part by the knowledge that no scheme of reform which had yet been advanced would be acceptable to all minorities.

New elections to the State Council were held in 1936. This time there was no boycott, and the Ceylon Tamil representation was increased from three to eight. No Moslem was elected, but this was remedied when the governor increased from one to two the number of Moslems in the eight seats filled by nomination. Once the State Council had been constituted, its first task was to divide into seven executive committees and proceed to the election of the chairmen who would then constitute the Board of Ministers. By a well-planned manœuvre, but to the surprise of many people, the State Council elected as ministers only those who belonged to the Sinhalese community, whereas in the previous State Council two of the ministerial posts had gone to the minority communities.

There was an immediate outcry from the minorities. They pointed out that they had only accepted the Donoughmore Constitution with the gravest misgivings and had opposed further reform because of their fear of being excluded from office. The Sinhalese replied that they wanted to convince the minorities of the defects of the constitution by demonstrating that it offered no real safeguards for the minorities. In any case, they added, the Secretary of State had said that he would only consider reform if the Board of Ministers put forward a scheme which carried unanimous support, and ministerial unanimity would now be easy to secure.

The new Board of Ministers, indeed, immediately renewed their demands for reform. Sir Edward Stubbs, the governor, was unable to accept all the suggestions advanced by the ministers, but he was of the opinion that the Donoughmore Constitution was by that time "a proved failure". Towards the end of 1937 the Secretary of State, Mr. Ormsby-Gore (later Lord Harlech), asked the new Governor of Ceylon, Sir Andrew Caldecott, to submit recommendations for constitutional reform after he had had an opportunity of acquainting himself with the views of different sections of opinion.

Caldecott's recommendations were embodied in what came to be known as the "Reforms Despatch". It was a most important document, "written with a vigour and directness unusual in official documents," as the Soulbury Commission's Report puts it. Caldecott recommended that there should be no curtailment of the governor's powers and no change in the franchise. He was, however, opposed to the Executive Committee system and recommended its replacement by what he called "a cabinet of the normal type".

The "Reforms Despatch" was published in December 1938, and fully discussed in Ceylon. The discussions revealed wide differences of view, and with the outbreak of war in Europe in 1939 it became evident that constitutional reform

would be delayed. The Ceylonese leaders were naturally concerned that no definite statement of the British attitude had
been made, but in September 1941 the British Government
communicated a statement to the Board of Ministers in Ceylon
in which they promised that "the question of constitutional
reform in Ceylon . . . will be taken up with the least possible
delay after the war".

The Ceylonese politicians were dissatisfied that the delay
contemplated was for an indefinite period and might be pro-
tracted, and in March 1942 the State Council asked that Sir
Stafford Cripps, who was to visit India to discuss the constitutional position there, should either visit Ceylon or receive
a deputation in India on the island's request for a declaration
that dominion status should be granted after the war. Although
this request was refused, a further statement from the British
Government was issued in May 1943 promising that "the post-
war re-examination of the reform of the Ceylon Constitution
. . . will be directed towards the grant to Ceylon . . . of full
responsible government under the Crown in all matters of
internal civil administration". Britain would retain control over
defence and external relations, and certain classes of Bills
would continue to be reserved. The Board of Ministers was
invited to draft a plan which, if approved by three-quarters of
the members of the State Council, would be examined "by
suitable commission or conference" after the war.

In February 1944 the proposals of the ministers were submitted to the Secretary of State. The main provision, as will
be noted later, was for the creation of a new and enlarged
state council and a cabinet system on the British model with
full ministerial responsibility.

At this point a serious difference of opinion arose between
the British Government and the leading politicians in Ceylon.
The Secretary of State announced in July 1944 that, in accordance with the statement of 1943, a commission would visit
Ceylon to "provide full opportunity for consultation to take
place with the various interests, including the minority communities, concerned with the subject of constitutional reform
in Ceylon, and with the proposals which the ministers have
formulated".

The ministers, rightly or wrongly, regarded this as a breach of the Declaration of 1943. They held that the sole function of the proposed commission should be an examination of their own proposals, and they therefore decided not to assist the commission, and in August formally withdrew their draft constitution. In March 1945, while the commission was completing its investigations in Ceylon, a Bill designed to confer immediate dominion status passed its third reading in the State Council by forty votes to seven. The Royal Assent was refused on the advice of the Secretary of State, Colonel Oliver Stanley.

The commission, under the chairmanship of Lord Soulbury, was in Ceylon from December 1944 to April 1945. It had before it the ministers' proposals which had been submitted to the Secretary of State early in 1944. Of the various other proposals which were put forward for discussion, perhaps the most interesting was a Tamil plan for 'balanced representation'— the 'Fifty-fifty Scheme', as it came to be called. This plan was not intended to interfere with the constitutional advances proposed by the ministers. Its main purpose was to prevent any one community securing a dominant position in the legislature. This was to be achieved by providing that half the seats in the legislature were filled by Sinhalese and the other half by the different minority communities. This would have meant that the Sinhalese were under-represented in the legislature. But the main objection to the plan was that it was communal representation under another name. To return to the system of communal representation, which had been abandoned some years earlier on the advice of the Donoughmore Commission, would have been a retrograde step.

The Indian Tamils supported the 'Fifty-fifty Scheme', but their main concern was with the franchise provisions. The difficulty, as has been noted earlier, was that many Indians were transient estate workers with no 'abiding interest' in Ceylon. The Sinhalese, rather naturally, were not willing to agree to full rights of citizenship being given to temporary residents. The problem was discussed fully by the ministers and argued before the Soulbury Commissioners. In the end both ministers and commissioners decided to make no immediate change in the franchise provisions then existing.

The Report of the Soulbury Commission was published in September 1945, and accorded substantially with the ministers' proposals. The main recommendations were as follows.

The executive committee system and the Board of Ministers were to be abolished and replaced by a cabinet of ministers responsible to an elected legislature, one member of which would be appointed prime minister: other ministers and parliamentary secretaries would be appointed on the recommendation of the prime minister.

The first chamber would consist of ninety-five elected members and six nominees of the governor-general. There would be a second chamber of thirty members, half being elected by members of the first chamber in accordance with the system of proportional representation by means of the single transferable vote, and half being persons chosen by the governor-general at his discretion.

There was to be a governor-general who would have overriding powers with respect to external affairs, defence, and certain other matters.

The three officers of state were to be abolished. The governor-general would appoint members to a public services commission, a judicial services commission, the chief justice, and judges of the supreme court. Universal suffrage would be retained.

These recommendations followed very largely the constitutional proposals of the ministers, but one important difference should be noted. The Soulbury Commission recommended the creation of a bicameral legislature: the ministers, on the other hand, had come to the conclusion that the question of a second chamber was so controversial that a 75 per cent majority could not be obtained for any such plan. They therefore decided to retain a unicameral legislature and to authorize it to establish a second chamber by ordinary legislation. As there was no reference to franchise in the ministers' proposals, it was assumed that they had not contemplated any immediate change.

In July 1945 Mr. Senanayake visited London at the invitation of the Secretary of State. The Soulbury Report had not yet been published. Soon after Mr. Senanayake's arrival in

London the result of the British general election became known, and Mr. George (later Lord) Hall succeeded Colonel Oliver Stanley as Secretary of State. Mr. Senanayake formulated and presented a plan for dominion status, together with proposed agreements between the United Kingdom and Ceylon on defence and external affairs.

In September the Soulbury Report was published, and the following month the decision of the British Government was announced. "His Majesty's Government are in sympathy with the desire of the people of Ceylon to advance towards dominion status and . . . have reached the conclusion that a constitution on the general lines proposed by the Soulbury Commission . . . will provide a workable basis for constitutional progress. . . ." After lengthy debate the British Government's proposals were accepted by the Ceylon State Council by fifty-one votes to three. Of the three who opposed this, two were Indian members and one a Sinhalese: three minority members were not present.

The new constitution was therefore introduced. A census was held in Ceylon in March 1946, electoral areas were delimited, and a general election took place. The victorious party, with forty-two seats in the lower chamber, was the United National Party (U.N.P.), a non-communal party of moderate views which had been formed by the amalgamation of the Sinhala Maha Sabha (Buddhist), the Ceylon Moslem League, the Ceylon National Congress, and the personal followers of Mr. Senanayake. The Opposition consisted of three Marxist parties, the Lanka Sama Samaj (Trotskyite) which won ten seats, the Bolshevik-Leninist Party, which won five seats, and the Communist Party (Stalinist) which won three seats and was later joined by two persons who had been elected as Independents; the Ceylon Tamil Congress, a communal party, which secured seven seats; and the Ceylon Indian Congress, with six seats. Twenty-one Independents were elected, and one representative of Labour.

Mr. D. S. Senanayake, the leader of the U.N.P. and Ceylon's first Prime Minister, had meanwhile renewed his demand for dominion status which—it was thought—was only held up pending a settlement in India. In June 1947 Mr. Creech Jones, the new Secretary of State, made the announcement for which Ceylon had been anxiously waiting. The constitution, he said, was to be amended so as to confer upon Ceylon "fully responsible status within the British Commonwealth". It was significant that the term 'dominion', with its suggestion of over-lordship, was not used. The British Government had, in effect, accepted the proposals which Mr. Senanayake had put forward in 1945.

The proposed alterations to the Ceylon Constitution were as follows:

(a) In place of the governor there would be a governor-general who, in the exercise of his powers, authorities and functions, would as far as may be act "in accordance with the constitutional conventions applicable to the exercise of similar powers, authorities and functions in the United Kingdom by His Majesty";

(b) the powers reserved to His Majesty to make laws for Ceylon in matters relating to defence and external affairs would be abolished;

(c) the provisions for the reservation of bills for His Majesty's pleasure would be revoked.

In addition, details were published of agreements between the United Kingdom and Ceylon Governments, relating to defence, external affairs, and public officers.

The Ceylon Independence Bill was presented to the British House of Commons on 13th November, and within a period of four weeks had passed both Houses of Parliament and received the Royal Assent.

The Ceylon Independence Act, 1947, extended to Ceylon the provisions of the Statute of Westminster by conferring on the Ceylon Parliament full legislative powers and depriving the United Kingdom of responsibility for the government of Ceylon. Its most significant provisions were as follows:

"No Act of the Parliament of the United Kingdom . . . shall extend, or be deemed to extend, to Ceylon as part of the law of Ceylon, unless it is expressly declared in that Act that Ceylon has requested, and consented to, the enactment thereof. . . . His Majesty's Government in the United Kingdom shall have no responsibility for the government of Ceylon. . . . No law and no provision of any law made after the appointed day by the Parliament of Ceylon shall be void or inoperative on the ground that it is repugnant to the law of England, or to the provisions of any existing or future Act of Parliament of the United Kingdom. . . ."

The Ceylon House of Representatives supported by fifty-nine votes to eleven the action taken by Mr. Senanayake to secure his country's independence: the voting in the Senate was twenty-one to five in support of Mr. Senanayake.

The Ceylon Independence Bill was supported by the U.N.P. but opposed by the Marxist parties and by the Tamil Congress and the Indian Congress, though for different reasons. The opposition of the Tamil and Indian parties to the Independence Bill was based on their fear that the constitution did not sufficiently safeguard the position of the minorities. In practice, the increasing sense of political responsibility which has been evident since independence has led to a lessening of communal differences. The majority of Tamils have come to the view that their real political enemy is not the Government but the Marxists, and in September 1948 the leader of the Tamil Congress agreed to join the Cabinet. His decision did not have the unanimous support of his party and a few members, including the party secretary, resigned their membership. The Indian Congress remains uncomfortably sandwiched between the Government and the Marxist parties.

The Marxists have taken the view that self-government within the British Commonwealth is a 'fake' and that only complete secession will give Ceylon real independence. The Russian veto of Ceylon's application for membership of the United Nations has been regarded by the Marxists in Ceylon as further proof that 'independence' is illusory. Ceylon can, of course, leave the Commonwealth at any time she wishes by the decision of her own Government, but, except among the Marxists and a few other extremists, there is no disposition to take this step.

L

CHAPTER XII

CEYLON AND THE FUTURE

"Difficulties are things that show what men are."—
Epictetus.

THE period of political struggle which culminated in the achievement of independence absorbed the energies of the majority of thinking Ceylonese. It was argued that problems of economic development and social welfare depended on a prior solution of the political problem. This was an understandable attitude which accorded well with western democratic theory. But its inevitable consequence was to create an unreal barrier between the nationalist and the reformer. The latter appeared in many guises—as official, businessman, missionary—and in all of them he was criticized for putting the cart before the horse. It was not that the nationalist politician was uninterested in the framing or administration of the nation's laws. In one sense, indeed, he was obsessed with the details of legislation and administration. A disproportionate part of the time of the legislatures of Ceylon between the two world wars was spent in discussing questions of detail. This was in part the result of a system which for so long had provided insufficient opportunities for educated Ceylonese to share in the major matters of national policy.

There was, then, a dichotomy of the minds of the Ceylonese leaders—a great interest in administrative details and at the same time a feeling that ameliorative legislation was hindering a solution of the urgent political problem.

The partial neglect of economic and social reform had the consequence that when the Second World War ended and Ceylon was on the brink of self-government, a number of serious unsolved problems required tackling. They had, in part, been masked by the artificial prosperity of the war. The Government of Mr. Senanayake was, therefore, faced with these difficulties immediately after it had taken office. What, briefly, were the economic and social problems?

Perhaps the most serious economic problem was the uncertain price in the world markets of the main exports—tea, rubber and coco-nut and coco-nut products. Whereas average export prices trebled between 1938 and 1948, import prices more than quadrupled in the same period. Since the war Ceylon has been increasing the volume of exports at a much greater rate than the volume of imports, but even so the balance of trade for 1948 showed a deficit of nearly £4 million. Yet it should be noted that Ceylon was in 1948 the only independent member of the Commonwealth to earn a net surplus of dollars.

The Ceylon Government considers that the long-term solution of the problem of export prices depends to a large extent on a diversification of the national economy so that the country is no longer dependent on the export of a very few staple commodities. The first step in this programme is to be an attempt to increase the quantity of foodstuffs grown in Ceylon. Foodstuffs normally constitute nearly half Ceylon's imports.

That the production of food can be increased by improved agricultural methods is evident from the following approximate figures of the annual yield of paddy per acre of cultivated land in a number of countries:

Italy	.. ..	4,000 lb.
Egypt	.. ..	3,000 ,,
Java	.. ..	2,000 ,,
India	.. ..	1,200 ,,
Ceylon	.. ..	500 ,,

In addition to increasing the yield from land already cultivated, an effort is being made to develop new agricultural land. It has been estimated that in time the area of land under productive cultivation can be twice the present cultivated area.

Three methods are being used to increase the production of food: the setting up by the Government of centres from which peasants can be given advice in scientific agricultural methods, the improvement and extension of scientific irrigation, and the expansion of agricultural co-operatives and the granting of credits. There were in 1946 over 6,000 co-operative societies with a membership of over one million.

Efforts are also being made to start new industries, but for many years to come industry cannot rival agriculture as a source of wealth. In any case, large-scale industrialization by the construction of factories should not be permitted to swamp cottage industries, such as textile weaving, coir spinning and weaving, and pottery manufacture, which have always been an important feature of the economy of Ceylon.

The two main social problems in Ceylon after the war were education and health: they were, of course, inter-related.

In theory there is free, compulsory education from six to fourteen years, but in reality fewer than half the children of school age attend school regularly. It has been estimated that in 1947 about one million children (about 60 per cent of those of school age) were actually on the school registers, and that only three-quarters of these normally attended. Although 62 per cent of the men are literate (1946), the figure for women is only 38 per cent.

Turning to health problems, it is significant that the most serious threats to the health of the people are all 'preventable' in the sense that the means of their elimination are known. At the top of the list should be placed malnutrition. It is difficult to measure the extent of malnutrition. It is only rarely that it is a direct cause of death: it usually weakens and debilitates the physique and increases the likelihood of disease. Furthermore, there is no recognized dietary standard which can be used to measure the extent of malnutrition. But it was estimated in 1941 that 35 per cent of the rural population consumed a diet deficient in calories, and that 26 per cent were on the border-line.

Malaria is another scourge. Approximately half the population was until recently under treatment for this disease. Malaria can be eradicated by preventing the breeding of anophelene mosquitoes, but this is a task which cannot be accomplished solely by governmental action: the co-operation of the citizen is necessary, and this depends on better education and the growth of a social conscience. The use of D.D.T. has now reduced the incidence of malaria very greatly, and the

World Health Organization has been asked to help in a malaria-eradication campaign.

A third source of ill-health and misery can be found in the various water-borne diseases such as hookworm, round-worm and dysentery. About a third of the population is under treatment for hookworm, and the intestinal diseases cause over 15,000 deaths a year. Water-borne diseases are less of a menace in the towns where piped water supplies and reliable sewerage systems can be provided. In rural areas it is much more difficult. Four out of five villages in Ceylon draw their water from wells, and it is the exception rather than the rule for wells to be properly protected.

It will be evident that the primary health problem in Ceylon will not be solved solely by providing hospitals, dispensaries, or clinics, or by training more doctors and nurses. Remedial action of this kind is necessary, but much more important is the improvement of social conditions, the spread of education, the elimination of superstition, the growth of a social conscience, an increase in living standards.

Apart from these economic and social questions, the Government faced a number of problems in connection with the minority communities. Since the abolition of communal representation on the recommendation of the Donoughmore Commission, communal hostility had declined but not disappeared. The majority of Sinhalese and Ceylon Tamils have supported the Government of Mr. Senanayake, but the Indians are still not satisfied with their position.

The relation of Ceylon to the neighbouring continent of India has always been a matter of importance. The vast majority of the inhabitants of the island either came from India themselves or are descended from those who once came from India. In a sense Ceylon was for long a pawn in the struggle of European nations which fought each other to decide who should be master of India. After the British conquest, Ceylon had at first been administered as if it were part of India, and there were always some Indians who claimed that historically Ceylon ought to be regarded as part of India and eventually should be united with the homeland. Even as late as 1945 Mr. Nehru had urged that Ceylon should join an Indian Federation since she was "culturally, racially and linguistically as much a part of India as any province of India". By 1949, however, Nehru had abandoned this position. Speaking at a press conference in New Delhi on 11th May, 1949, he said:

> "We are quite happy that Ceylon is a completely independent entity. We do not, in any sense, desire any closer association with Ceylon than that which exists today. I want to make this perfectly clear, because there has been some misapprehension in the minds of the people and the Government of Ceylon that we have some designs upon them. We have no designs at all. There is no possibility of our trying to make Ceylon, in any sense, a part of India."

Ceylon has played a significant role in Commonwealth affairs. A Conference of Commonwealth Foreign Ministers was held in Colombo in 1949. Ceylon's membership of the United Nations was prevented by the veto of the Soviet Union, but Ceylon has participated in the work of a number of the specialized agencies such as the Food and Agriculture Organization, the World Health Organization, the International Labour Organization, and the United Nations Educational, Scientific and Cultural Organization.

Whatever may be said in criticism of the policy of the present Government, the fact remains that it has tackled Ceylon's problems with vigour and enthusiasm. Although some of its members, including the Prime Minister, were imprisoned as political offenders by the British authorities during the First World War, there is today no trace of hostility or bitterness between the Governments of the United Kingdom and Ceylon. The first Parliament of independent Ceylon was opened by the Duke of Gloucester in February 1948. There are close ties between the Westminster and Colombo Parliaments. The British House of Commons has presented to the House of Representatives in Ceylon a Speaker's chair and mace. The procedure in the Colombo Parliament is similar to that at Westminster. After a century and a half of British colonial status, Ceylon became in 1948 the youngest—and the smallest— independent country in the Commonwealth.

HISTORY OF CEYLON

A Select Bibliography

THE CHRONICLES

1. The *Dipavamsa*. Edited and translated by Hermann Oldenberg. London, Edinburgh: Williams and Norgate. 1879.
   (The *Dipavamsa* is a chronicle in verse, probably composed about the fourth century A.D.)
2. The *Mahavamsa*. Translated by Wilhelm Geiger and Mabel Haynes Brode. Oxford University Press for the Pali Text Society. 1912.
   (The *Mahavamsa* is an epic history compiled by Buddhist chroniclers about the sixth century A.D. It is the chief source of information on the early period.)
3. The *Culavamsa*. Translated by Wilhelm Geiger and C. Mabel Rickmers. Oxford University Press for the Pali Text Society. Two volumes. 1929–30.
   (The *Culavamsa* continues the *Mahavamsa* from the fourth century until 1815. It was composed at different times after the thirteenth century.)
4. The *Rajavaliya*. Translated by B. Gunasekara. Colombo: Ceylon Government Printer. 1900.
   (The *Rajavaliya* is a historical narrative of the Sinhalese kings and was probably composed towards the end of the seventeenth century. Though less reliable than the *Mahavamsa* and the *Culavamsa*, it is a useful source.)

CHAPTERS II—III

THE ARRIVAL OF THE SINHALESE AND THE TAMIL INVASIONS

5. Mendis, G. C. *The Early History of Ceylon*. Calcutta: Y.M.C.A. Publishing House. Ninth impression. 1948.

CHAPTER IV

THE PORTUGUESE PERIOD

6. Barros, João de. *History of Ceylon to* A.D. *1600*. Translated and edited by Donald Ferguson. Colombo: Ceylon Government Printer. 1909.

 (Barros was a Portuguese historian of the sixteenth century: his record of events puts the best interpretation on the acts of his countrymen.)

7. Couto, Diogo de. *History of Ceylon to* A.D. *1600*. Translated and edited by Donald Ferguson. Colombo: Ceylon Government Printer. 1909.

 (Couto continued the record, begun by Barros, of Portuguese expansion.)

8. Pieris, P. E. *Ceylon, 1505–1658*. Colombo, London: Times of Ceylon Co. Ltd. 1923.

9. Pieris, P. E. *Ceylon: the Portuguese Era*. Colombo: the Colombo Apothecaries Co. Two volumes. 1913–14.

10. Pieris, P. E. *Ceylon and the Portuguese, 1505–1658*. Tellippalai: American Ceylon Mission Press. 1920.

11. Queyroz, Fernão de. *The Temporal and Spiritual Conquest of Ceylon*. Translated by S. G. Perera. Colombo: Ceylon Government Printer. 1930.

 (This is the best contemporary account of the Portuguese period. Father Queyroz was a Jesuit who lived in India from 1635 until his death in 1688. His book is based on the published works of Portuguese historians like João de Barros, Diogo de Couto, João Rodriguez de Sa y Menezes, and Manoel Faria y Souza, as well as on unpublished manuscripts and reminiscences of personal friends and acquaintances familiar with Ceylon.)

12. Ribeiro, João. *History of Ceylon*. Translated from the Portuguese by P. E. Pieris. Colombo: the Colombo Apothecaries Co. Ltd. Second edition. 1909. (Includes a few English extracts of Barros and Couto.)

 Translated by George Lee from the French translation by Abbé le Grand of the Portuguese original. Colombo: Ceylon Government Press. 1847.

 (Captain Ribeiro served in the Portuguese Army in Ceylon from 1640 until the Dutch capture of Colombo in 1658.)

CHAPTER V

THE DUTCH PERIOD

13. Baldæus, Philip. *A True and Exact Description of the Isle of Ceylon.* Printed at Amsterdam. 1672. English translation included in Vol. III of Churchill's *A Collection of Voyages and Travels.* Third edition. London. 1745.
(Baldæus was a Dutch Minister in Ceylon in the early years of the Dutch occupation.)

14. Becker, Hendrik. *Memoirs and Instructions of Dutch Governors, Commanders,* etc. Translated by Sophia Anthonisz. Colombo: Ceylon Government Printer. 1914.

15. Goens, Ryclof van. *Memoir.* Translated by Sophia Pieters. Colombo: Ceylon Government Printer. 1910.

16. Haafner, Jacques. *Travels on Foot Through the Island of Ceylon.* Translated from the Dutch. London: Sir Richard Phillips and Co. 1821.
(Haafner served for some years in the Dutch East India Company and visited Ceylon about the year 1782.)

17. Heere, Gerrit de. *Diary.* Translated by Sophia Anthonisz. Colombo: Ceylon Government Printer. 1914.

18. Imhoff, Gustaaf Willem van. *Report on the Administration of Ceylon.* Translated by Sophia Pieters. Colombo: Ceylon Government Press. 1911. Condensed English translation printed as an Appendix to Riberio, *q.v.*

19. *Instructions from the Governor-General and Council of India to the Governor of Ceylon, 1656–65.* Translated by Sophia Pieters. Colombo: Ceylon Government Printer. 1908.

20. Knox, Robert. *An Historical Relation of the Island of Ceylon.* First published in London in 1681. Selections edited by E. F. C. Ludowyk under the title *Robert Knox in the Kandyan Kingdom.* Oxford University Press. 1950.

21. Mooyaart, Anthony. *Memoir.* Translated by Sophia Pieters. Colombo: Ceylon Government Press. 1910.

22. Pielat, Jacob Christian. *Memoir.* Translated by Sophia Pieters. Colombo: Ceylon Government Printer. 1905.

23. Pieris, P. E. *Ceylon and the Hollanders, 1658–1796.* Tellippalai: American Ceylon Mission Press. 1918.

24. Rhee, Thomas van. *Memoir.* Translated by Sophia Anthonisz. Colombo: Ceylon Government Press. 1915.

25. Schreuder, Jan. *Memoir*. Condensed English translation printed as an Appendix to Ribeiro, *q.v.*
26. Simons, Cornelius Jan. *Memoir*. Translated by Sophia Anthonisz. Colombo: Ceylon Government Press. 1914.
27. Zwaardecroon, Hendrik. *Memoir*. Translated by Sophia Pieters. Colombo: Ceylon Government Press. 1911.

CHAPTERS VI—XI

THE BRITISH PERIOD

28. Annesley, George, *Viscount Valentia. Voyages and Travels to India, Ceylon, the Red Sea, Abyssinia, and Egypt.* Four volumes (Vol. I deals with Ceylon). London: F. C. and J. Rivington. 1811.
    (Lord Valentia was a careful observer. His account of North's relations with Kandy is especially useful.)
29. Bertolacci, Anthony. *View of the Agricultural, Commercial, and Financial Interests of Ceylon.* London: Black, Parbury, and Allen. 1817.
    (Bertolacci, a Corsican by birth, was a protégé of North and served in Ceylon from 1798 to 1814. This book is a valuable and accurate account of the economy of Ceylon at the beginning of the nineteenth century. It includes a wealth of statistical material, a description of the complicated land tenure system, a note on the organization of the public service, and an account of the laws and customs of Kandy as described to the Dutch Governor Falk by some leading priests in 1769.)
30. Boyd, Hugh. *Embassy to Kandy*. This forms Vol. II of Boyd's *Miscellaneous Works*, edited by Lawrence Dundas Campbell. London: Cadell and Davies. 1800.
31. Collins, *Sir* Charles. *The Administration of Ceylon.* Royal Institute of International Affairs. 1951.
32. Cordiner, James. *A Description of Ceylon.* Two volumes. London. 1807.
    (Cordiner was chaplain to the garrison at Colombo from 1799 to 1804. He greatly admired Frederick North and dedicates the work to him. His account of the Kandyan war of 1803 is useful though he goes out of his way to exonerate North of all blame for the disaster.)
33. D'Oyly, *Sir* John. *A Sketch of the Constitution of the Kandyan Kingdom.* London. 1832.

34. Gregory, *Lady (editor)*. *Sir William Gregory*. London. 1894.
35. Haeckel, Ernst. *A Visit to Ceylon*. Translated by Clara Bell. London: Kegan Paul. 1883.
    (Haeckel, the German scientist, visited Ceylon in 1881–2.)
36. Jennings, *Sir* Ivor. *The Constitution of Ceylon*. Oxford University Press. Second Edition 1951.
    (Sir Ivor Jennings was closely associated in an unofficial capacity with the negotiations which led up to the attainment of independence in 1948.)
37. Jennings, *Sir* Ivor. *The Economy of Ceylon*. Oxford University Press. 1948.
38. Jennings, *Sir* Ivor. *Nationalism and Political Development in Ceylon*. New York: Institute of Pacific Relations. 1950.
    (Mimeographed.)
39. Lord, Walter Trewen. *Sir Thomas Maitland*. London: T. Fisher Unwin. 1897.
40. Mills, Lennox A. *Ceylon under British Rule, 1795–1932*. Oxford University Press. 1933.
    (Contains a useful bibliography.)
41. Namasivayam, S. *The Legislatures of Ceylon*. Faber & Faber. 1951.
42. Neil, The Rev. William *(editor)*. *The Cleghorn Papers*. A. and C. Black. 1927.
    (Hugh Cleghorn was employed in the British Secret Service in Ceylon from 1793–7 and was the first Colonial Secretary of Ceylon.)
43. Percival, Robert. *An Account of the Island of Ceylon*. Second edition. London: C. and R. Baldwin. 1805.
44. Pieris, P. E. *Tri Sinhala*. Cambridge: Heffer. Colombo: The Colombo Apothecaries Co., Ltd. 1939.
45. Pybus, John. *An Account of a Mission to the King of Kandy in 1762*. Colombo: Ceylon Government Printer. 1862.
46. Quincey, Thomas de. *Ceylon*. Included in Vol. XI of *Collected Works*. Edinburgh: A. and C. Black. 1863.
47. Silva, Colvin R. de. *Ceylon under British Occupation, 1795–1833: Its Political, Administrative and Economic Development*. Two volumes. Colombo: The Colombo Apothecaries Co., Ltd. 1942.
48. Skinner, Thomas. *Fifty Years in Ceylon*. Edited by Annie Skinner. London: W. H. Allen & Co. Ltd. 1891.
49. Tennent, James Emerson. *Ceylon*. London: Longmans, Green. Two volumes. 1859.
    (Tennent was Civil Secretary to the Ceylon Government

from 1845–50. Though first published almost a century ago, his book remains an invaluable source of information.)
50. Turner, L. J. B. *The History of the Maritime Provinces, 1795–1803.*

OFFICIAL PUBLICATIONS

51. *Report of Lt.-Col. Colebrooke Upon the Revenues and the Administration of the Government of Ceylon.* 1831–2.
52. *Report of Charles Hay Cameron Upon the Judicial Establishments and Procedure in Ceylon.* 1832.
53. *Ceylon: Papers Relative to the Affairs of Ceylon.* Printed by W. Clowes and Sons for Her Majesty's Stationery Office. 1849.
54. *First, Second and Third Reports of the Select Committee on Ceylon and British Guiana.* 1849.
55. *First, Second and Third Reports from the Select Committee on Ceylon; Together with the Proceedings of the Committee, Minutes of Evidence. . . .* 1850–1.
56. *Ceylon: Report of the Special Commission on the Constitution.* (The Donoughmore Report.) (Cmd. 3131.) His Majesty's Stationery Office. 1928.
57. *Ceylon: Report of the Commission on Constitutional Reform.* (The Soulbury Report.) (Cmd. 6677.) His Majesty's Stationery Office. 1945.
58. The Independence of Ceylon. Sessional paper XXII–1947. Colombo: Ceylon Government Press. 1947.
59. Ceylon Independence Act, 1947. (11 Geo. 6, 1947–8, ch. 7.) His Majesty's Stationery Office. 1947.
60. The Constitution of Ceylon. Sessional paper III–1948. Colombo: Ceylon Government Press. 1948.
61. Ceylon Year Book, 1948. Colombo: Ceylon Government Press. 1948.

MISCELLANEOUS

62. Seligman, C. G. and Brenda Z. *The Veddas.* Cambridge University Press. 1911.

INDEX

165

For Product Safety Concerns and Information please contact our EU
representative GPSR@taylorandfrancis.com
Taylor & Francis Verlag GmbH, Kaufingerstraße 24, 80331 München, Germany